Contents

Getting the most from this book

Examiner tips

Advice from the examiner on key points in the text to help you learn and recall unit content, avoid pitfalls, and polish your exam technique in order to boost your grade.

Knowledge check

Rapid-fire questions throughout the Content Guidance section to check your understanding.

Knowledge check answers

1 Turn to the back of the book for the Knowledge check answers.

Summary

Summaries

- Each core topic is rounded off by a bullet-list summary for quick-check reference of what you need to know.

Questions & Answers

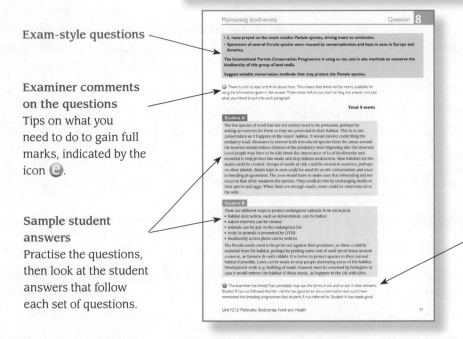

Exam-style questions

Examiner comments on the questions
Tips on what you need to do to gain full marks, indicated by the icon ⓔ.

Sample student answers
Practise the questions, then look at the student answers that follow each set of questions.

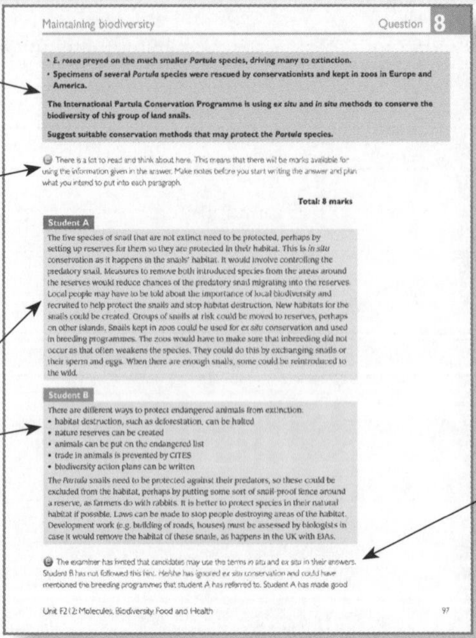

Maintaining biodiversity — Question 8

- ***E. rosea* preyed on the much smaller *Portula* species, driving many to extinction.**
- **Specimens of several *Portula* species were rescued by conservationists and kept in zoos in Europe and America.**

The International Partula Conservation Programme is using *ex situ* and *in situ* methods to conserve the biodiversity of this group of land snails.

Suggest suitable conservation methods that may protect the *Portula* species.

ⓔ There is a lot to read and think about here. This means that there will be marks available for using the information given in the answer. Make notes before you start writing the answer and plan what you intend to put into each paragraph.

Total: 8 marks

Student A

The five species of snail that are not extinct need to be protected, perhaps by setting up reserves for them so they are protected in their habitat. This is *in situ* conservation as it happens in the snails' habitat. It would involve controlling the predatory snail. Measures to remove both introduced species from the areas around the reserves would reduce chances of the predatory snail migrating into the reserves. Local people may have to be told about the importance of local biodiversity and recruited to help protect the snails and stop habitat destruction. New habitats for the snails could be created. Groups of snails at risk could be moved to reserves, perhaps on other islands. Snails kept in zoos could be used for *ex situ* conservation and used in breeding programmes. The zoos would have to make sure that inbreeding did not occur as that often weakens the species. They could do this by exchanging snails or their sperm and eggs. When there are enough snails, some could be reintroduced to the wild.

Student B

There are different ways to protect endangered animals from extinction:
- habitat destruction, such as deforestation, can be halted
- nature reserves can be created
- animals can be put on the endangered list
- trade in animals is prevented by CITES
- biodiversity action plans can be written

The *Portula* snails need to be protected against their predators, so these could be excluded from the habitat, perhaps by putting some sort of snail-proof fence around a reserve, as farmers do with rabbits. It is better to protect species in their natural habitat if possible. Laws can be made to stop people destroying areas of the habitat. Development work (e.g. building of roads, houses) must be assessed by biologists in case it would remove the habitat of these snails, as happens in the UK with EIAs.

ⓔ The examiner has hinted that candidates may use the terms *in situ* and *ex situ* in their answers. Student B has not followed this hint. He/she has ignored *ex situ* conservation and could have mentioned the breeding programmes that student A has referred to. Student A has made good

Unit F212: Molecules, Biodiversity, Food and Health 97

Examiner commentary on sample student answers
Find out how many marks each answer would be awarded in the exam and then read the examiner comments (preceded by the icon ⓔ) following each student answer.
Annotations that link back to points made in the student answers show exactly how and where marks are gained or lost.

STUDENT UNIT GUIDE

NEW EDITION

OCR AS Biology Unit F212

Molecules, Biodiversity, Food and Health

Richard Fosbery

PHILIP ALLAN

Philip Allan Updates, an imprint of Hodder Education, an Hachette UK company, Market Place, Deddington, Oxfordshire OX15 0SE

Orders
Bookpoint Ltd, 130 Milton Park, Abingdon, Oxfordshire OX14 4SB
tel: 01235 827827
fax: 01235 400401
e-mail: education@bookpoint.co.uk
Lines are open 9.00 a.m.–5.00 p.m., Monday to Saturday, with a 24-hour message answering service.
You can also order through the Philip Allan Updates website: www.philipallan.co.uk

ISBN 978-1-4441-6251-6

First printed 2012
Impression number 5 4 3 2
Year 2017 2016 2015 2014 2013

Cover image: norman blue/Fotolia

Printed in Dubai

P02009

About this book

This unit guide is the second of two that cover the OCR AS specification in biology. It is intended to help you prepare for **Unit F212: Molecules, Biodiversity, Food and Health**. It is divided into two sections:

- **Content Guidance** — here you will find key facts, key concepts and links with other parts of the AS/A2 biology course; you should find the **Focus on practical skills** sections useful for the practical work which is assessed in Unit F213. The **links** should help to show you how information in this unit is useful preparation for other units.
- **Questions and Answers** — these are questions covering the nine sections in Unit F212, together with answers written by two candidates and examiner's comments.

This is not just a revision aid. This is a guide to the whole unit and you can use it throughout the 2 years of your course if you decide to go on to A2. You will gain a much better understanding of the topics in Modules 2 and 3 of this unit if you read around the subject. I have suggested a variety of websites that you can use for extra information. These will help you especially with questions that include data or case studies. In some cases, you will find it very useful to have examples to quote in your answers. Do not forget to add any useful information you find to your notes.

The **Content Guidance** section will help you to:

- organise your notes and to check that you have highlighted the important points (key facts) — little 'chunks' of knowledge that you can remember
- check that you understand the links to practical work, since you will need your knowledge of this unit when doing the practical tasks in Unit F213: Practical Skills in Biology 1
- understand how these little 'chunks' fit into the wider picture; this will help:
  - to support Units F211 and F213 (you will find knowledge of this unit essential for F213 and it may be useful for F211)
  - to support the A2 units, if you decide to continue the course

You may be entered for F211 in January of your AS year, in which case, you will not have time to do any of this unit. However, many candidates do not take January examinations and so take the two units in June.

There is a Student Unit Guide specifically for the practical assessment in F213 and you will find some references to it in the sections entitled 'Focus on Practical Skills' in this guide for F212.

The **Questions and Answers** section will help you to:

- check the way the examiners ask questions at AS
- understand what the examiners mean by terms like 'explain' and 'describe'
- interpret the question material — especially any data that the examiners give you
- write concisely and answer the questions that the examiners set

AS biology

The diagram below shows you the three units that make up the AS course. You should have a copy of the specification for the whole of the course. Keep it in your file with your notes and refer to it constantly. You should know exactly which topics you have covered so far and how much more you have to do.

Unit F211		Unit F212		Unit F213
Cells, Exchange and Transport	+	Molecules, Biodiversity, Food and Health	+	Practical Skills in Biology 1

The specification outlines what you are expected to learn and do. The content of the specification is written as **learning outcomes**; these state what you should be able to do after studying and revising each topic. Some learning outcomes are very precise and cover just a small amount of factual information. Some are much broader. Do not think that any two learning outcomes will take exactly the same length of time to cover in class or during revision. Some of the learning outcomes deal with practical biology — in this guide these are covered in the **Focus on practical skills** sections. It is a good idea to write a glossary to the words in the learning outcomes; the examiners will expect you to know what they mean. This guide should help you to do this.

Units

Length

The units used are nm, µm, mm, m and km:

- 1000 nm (nanometres) = 1 µm (micrometre)
- 1000 µm = 1 mm (millimetre)
- 1000 mm = 1 m; 1000 m = 1 km

You may be expected to find the measurements or magnifications of cells in Units F212 and F213.

Volume

The units used are cm^3 and dm^3: 1000 cm^3 = 1 dm^3.

You will often find ml (millilitre) on glassware and in books. Examination papers, however, use cm^3 (cubic centimetre or 'centimetre cubed') and dm^3 (cubic decimetre or 'decimetre cubed'). 1 cm^3 is the same as 1 ml; 1 dm^3 is the same as 1 litre (1 l or 1 L). 1000 cm^3 = 1 dm^3.

In this guide you will come across volumes in the sections on biological molecules and enzymes.

Energy

The units used are joules (J), kilojoules (kJ) and megajoules (MJ):

- 1000 J = 1 kJ
- 1000 kJ = 1 MJ

The energy provided by your diet is given in kilojoules (or in megajoules). On packets of food and in books on diet you will often find energy as calories or kilocalories. These units are not used in examination papers.

Names of organisms

In this unit, you have to know about the binomial system for naming organisms. Throughout the book, organisms are given their common English names and their scientific names.

Content Guidance

Module 1: Biological molecules

Biological molecules

Water

Key concepts you must understand

We would expect water to be a gas at the temperatures on Earth. A heavier molecule with a similar formula, hydrogen sulfide (H_2S), is a gas. Most water is a liquid, rather than a gas, because of hydrogen bonding.

Key facts you must know

Water molecules are dipolar (two poles). The electrons that form the covalent bond between hydrogen and oxygen tend to remain closer to the oxygen atom, giving it a slight negative charge (indicated by δ–). The hydrogen atoms have a slight positive charge (δ+), which means they are attracted to oxygen atoms on adjacent water molecules. This weak attraction between hydrogen and oxygen is called a hydrogen bond. Hydrogen bonding in water molecules is shown in Figure 1.

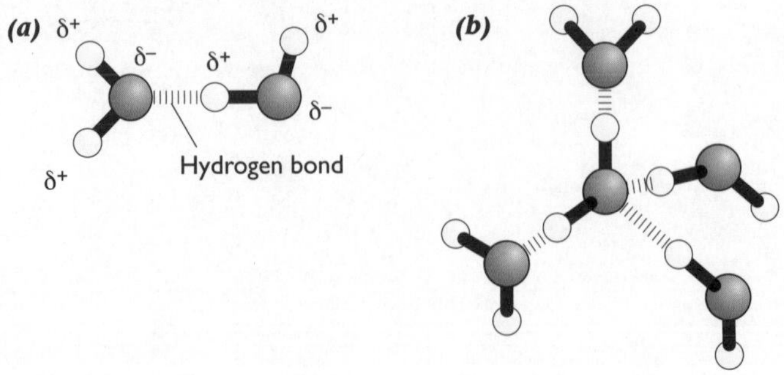

Figure 1 (a) Two water molecules with a hydrogen bond between them; (b) a cluster of water molecules held together by hydrogen bonds

Roles of water in organisms

Solvent action

Ions (e.g. sodium and chloride ions) and polar molecules (e.g. glucose and amino acids) are charged. They are attracted to water molecules because of the weak positive and negative 'poles' and are therefore dispersed easily in water, forming solutions. Water is a good solvent for ions and many biological molecules.

Examiner tip
Ions and polar molecules are important in biology. Make sure you understand why they are charged and how this makes them soluble in water.

Cohesion

Hydrogen bonds cause water molecules to 'stick together'. This makes it possible for them to travel up xylem vessels in plants in the transpiration stream (see Module 2 in the Student Unit Guide for Unit F211).

Latent heat of vaporisation

It takes energy to break hydrogen bonds between water molecules and convert liquid water to water vapour. So, when water evaporates from plants and animals, it cools them down.

Specific heat capacity

Water absorbs a significant amount of energy before it changes state, so the temperature does not change quickly.

Links

Hydrogen bonds are important in stabilising proteins, maintaining the structure of DNA and tRNA and forming strong molecules, such as cellulose and collagen. Before DNA can be replicated, hydrogen bonds between the two polynucleotide chains making up the double helix must be broken.

Amino acids and proteins

Key concepts you must understand

Proteins are unbranched macromolecules made of amino acids joined together by peptide bonds. Proteins are made from 20 different amino acids, which can be arranged in many different sequences. This gives a huge variety of different proteins, having many different functions.

Single chains of amino acids are polypeptides. These may be folded into complex three-dimensional (3D) shapes to form globular proteins, such as haemoglobin. Fibrous proteins, such as collagen, are made of polypeptides arranged in simpler shapes, such as helices.

Key facts you must know

Amino acids

The generalised structure of an amino acid is shown in Figure 2.

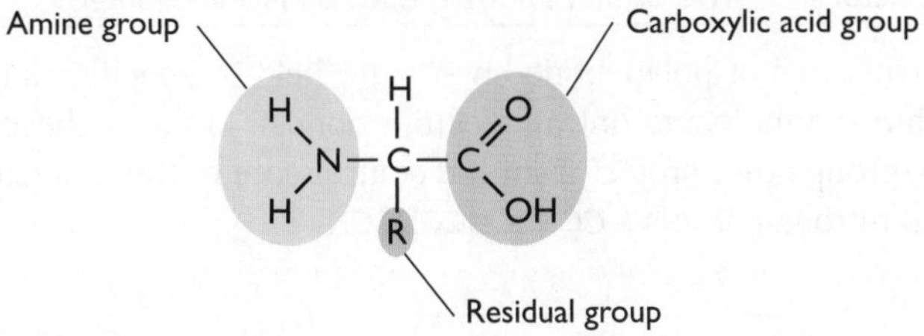

Figure 2 The generalised structure of an amino acid

Examiner tip
At a pH specific to each amino acid the molecule neither gains nor loses protons and carries no charge. In solutions with a pH lower than this, protons are accepted by the $-NH_2$ group, which becomes $-NH_3^+$. In solutions with a higher pH, protons are donated by the –COOH group, which becomes $-COO^-$.

Knowledge check 1
Explain why there are so many different types of proteins.

It is the R groups that make amino acids different from one another. Glycine (the simplest amino acid) has hydrogen as its R group. Alanine has $-CH_3$. Two amino acids are joined by a peptide bond that forms between the amine group of one amino acid and the carboxylic acid group of the other. This is a condensation reaction.

The formation and breakage of a peptide bond is shown in Figure 3.

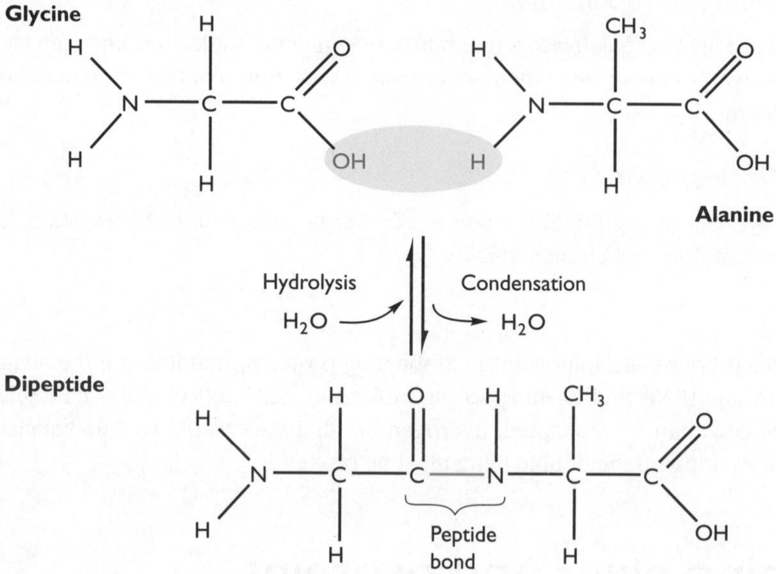

Figure 3 Formation and breakage of a peptide bond between glycine and alanine

Some proteins, such as the enzyme lipase, are made of one polypeptide; some are made of two or more. Haemoglobin, the enzyme catalase and many antibodies are made of four polypeptides. Levels of organisation in proteins refer to their structure. They are outlined in Table 1 and illustrated in Figure 4.

Table 1 Levels of organisation in proteins

Level of organisation	Structure
Primary structure	The sequence of amino acids in a polypeptide; amino acids are linked together by peptide bonds (also includes position of disulfide bonds)
Secondary structure	Polypeptide folded into an α-helix (a right-handed helix), or a β-pleated sheet. Secondary structure is stabilised by hydrogen bonds
Tertiary structure	Secondary structure folded to form complex 3D shape held together by a variety of bonds — see below
Quaternary structure	Two or more polypeptides arranged together

Examiner tip
Making tables is a good way to organise what you need to learn. Start a table to compare the structural features and roles of biological molecules (proteins, carbohydrates, lipids, and nucleic acids).

The tertiary structures of polypeptide chains are held in specific shapes by bonds that exist within the molecule (intramolecular bonds). Many of these bonds occur between the R groups that project from the central core of the molecule, formed by the carbon and nitrogen atoms (–CCNCCNCCNCCN– etc.).

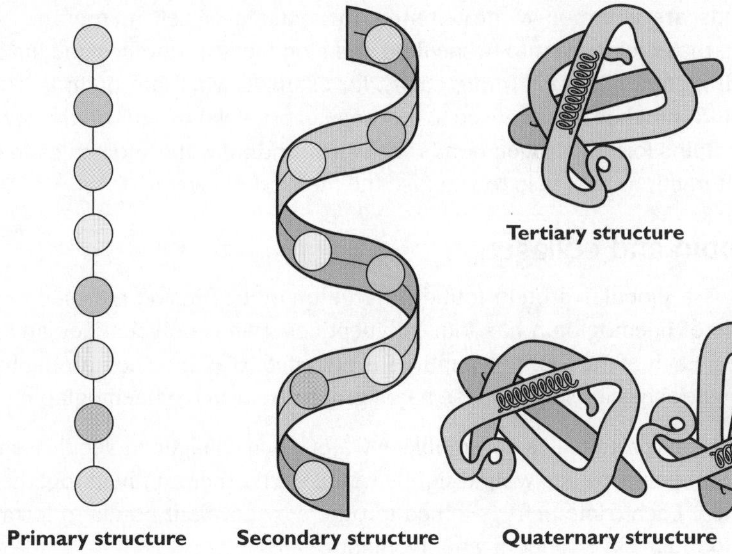

Figure 4 Levels of organisation in proteins

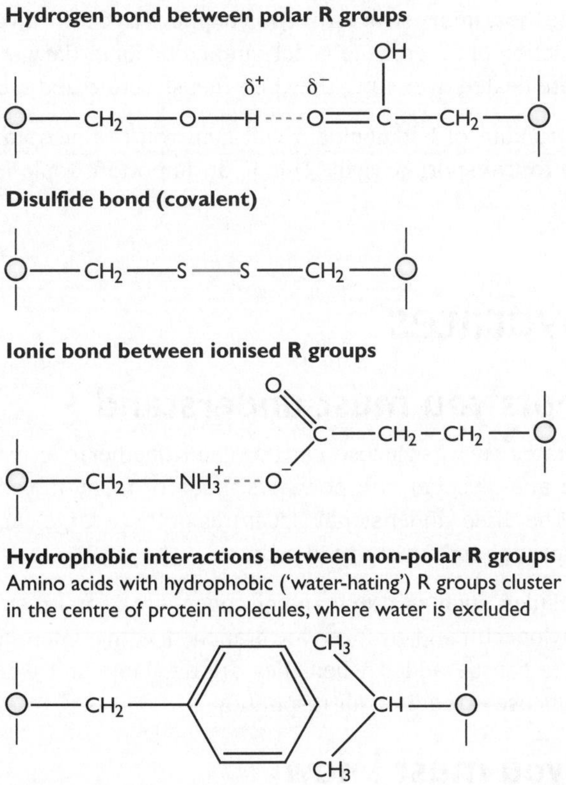

Figure 5 Intramolecular bonds that stabilise proteins

The disulfide bond is the strongest of these because it is a covalent bond. It is formed between R groups of the amino acid cysteine. The R group is –SH and when proteins are formed, these groups react to form the –S–S– bond shown in Figure 5.

Examiner tip

Use the internet to find models of protein structures. You should be able to find plenty of ribbon models that show α-helices; β-pleated sheets are depicted as broad arrows (see Figure 2 in Question 1 on page 71).

Disulfide bonds are common in proteins on the outside of cell membranes (e.g. receptors) and those released into tissue fluid and blood (e.g. antibodies and insulin). Ionic and hydrogen bonds break more easily, for example when a protein is heated above about 40°C or when it is exposed to a change in pH. Polar groups on the outside of globular proteins form hydrogen bonds with surrounding water molecules to give hydrophilic interactions that help to stabilise the molecule in water.

Haemoglobin and collagen

Examiner tip

Look at molecular models of haemoglobin and collagen to see how globular and fibrous proteins differ. Use what you find to help answer Knowledge check 2.

Knowledge check 2

Make a table to compare the structures and functions of haemoglobin and collagen.

Haemoglobin is a globular protein found in large quantities inside red blood cells. Each molecule of haemoglobin has four polypeptides: two α-polypeptides and two β-polypeptides. Each of the four polypeptides is attached to an iron-containing haem group. Oxygen attaches loosely to these haem groups to form oxyhaemoglobin.

Collagen is a fibrous protein. It is not soluble in water. Each collagen molecule is made of three identical polypeptides wound tightly round each other and held together by hydrogen bonds. Each triple helix is joined to others by covalent bonds to form the strong fibres found in skin, tendons and ligaments.

Links

Genes determine the primary structure of polypeptides (see the Unit Guide for F211). The specific function of an enzyme is determined by its tertiary structure. When most proteins are heated over 40°C, they lose this structure and are denatured.

Knowing the structure of haemoglobin will help you to understand the way in which it works to transport oxygen. This is an important topic in Module 2 of Unit F211.

Carbohydrates

Key concepts you must understand

Simple carbohydrates, such as glucose, can be joined together to form large molecules. Starch, cellulose and glycogen are polymers made of many molecules of glucose joined together. The three-dimensional structures of these large carbohydrates give them special properties and functions in cells.

Long-chain molecules, such as starch and glycogen, are good for storage since they are compact. Amylopectin and glycogen are branched, with numerous endings where glucose molecules can be added when they are available and where they can be removed when glucose is required for respiration.

Key facts you must know

Carbohydrates:

- contain hydrogen and oxygen in a ratio of 2:1, for example glucose, $C_6H_{12}O_6$
- have the general formula $C_x(H_2O)_y$ in which x may be three, four, five, six or seven

- include monosaccharides, sometimes known as simple sugars, e.g. glucose; disaccharides, also known as complex sugars, e.g. sucrose; and polysaccharides, e.g. starch (amylose and amylopectin), glycogen and cellulose

Glucose molecules exist in two forms: alpha (α) and beta (β) (Figure 6).

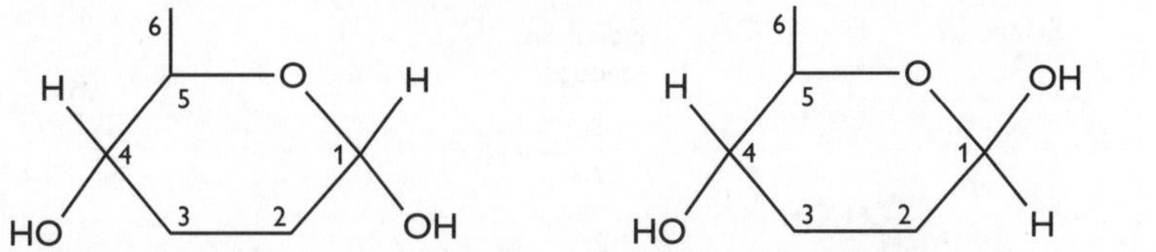

α-Glucose (note that the –H is above the –OH on carbon atom 1)

β-Glucose (note that the –OH is above the –H on carbon atom 1)

Figure 6

The difference between the two is small, yet polymers of these two forms of glucose show important differences.

Two α-glucose molecules are joined together to form maltose:

glucose + glucose → maltose

The glucose molecules are joined together by a glycosidic bond between carbon atom 1 on one glucose and carbon atom 4 on another. The bond is called a 1,4 glycosidic bond.

Figure 7 shows how glucose is joined with another simple sugar, fructose, to form sucrose:

glucose + fructose → sucrose

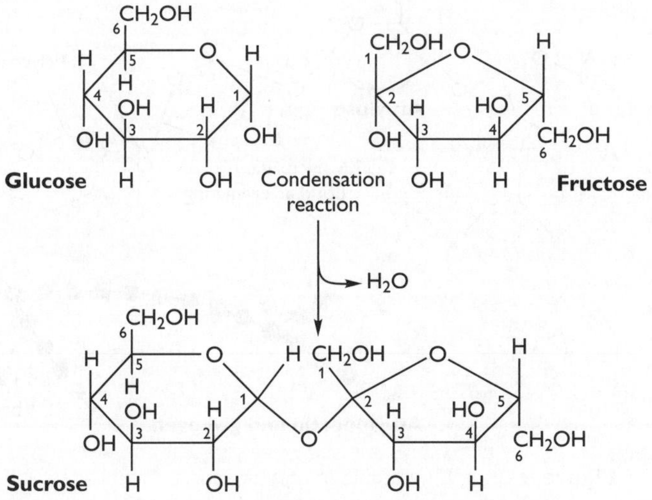

Figure 7 Forming a 1,2 glycosidic bond between glucose and fructose to form sucrose

This is a condensation reaction, because a molecule of water is formed.

Figure 8 shows the hydrolysis of sucrose to glucose and fructose. It is what happens when sucrose is boiled with hydrochloric acid.

Knowledge check 3

State how α-glucose differs from β-glucose.

Knowledge check 4

State three ways in which the structure of α-glucose shown in Figure 6 differs from the structure of a generalised amino acid (Figure 2).

Examiner tip

Condensation reactions are also known as dehydration reactions.

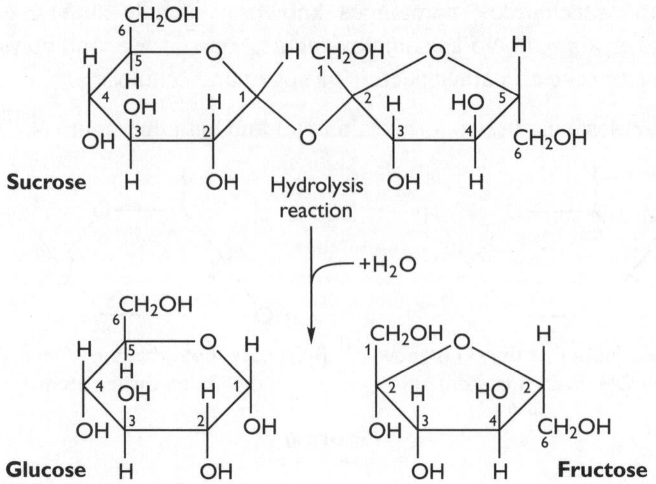

Figure 8 Breaking the glycosidic bond in sucrose to make glucose and fructose

The acid acts as a catalyst, speeding up the addition of water to break the glycosidic bond. Sucrose and maltose are disaccharides as they are composed of two simple sugar units joined together by a glycosidic bond.

Starch (amylose and amylopectin), glycogen and cellulose are polymers of glucose. They are made of many glucose molecules joined by glycosidic bonds. Amylose is formed when α-glucose monomers, joined by 1,4 glycosidic bonds, form a long chain with a compact helical structure. Amylopectin and glycogen are also polymers of α-glucose, but some of the glucose molecules are attached by 1,6 glycosidic bonds to form branching points (Figure 9).

Examiner tip

Figure 9 shows how the α-glucose molecules are arranged in amylose. Each β-glucose molecule in cellulose is arranged at 180° to those on either side. This is responsible for the straight chain structure.

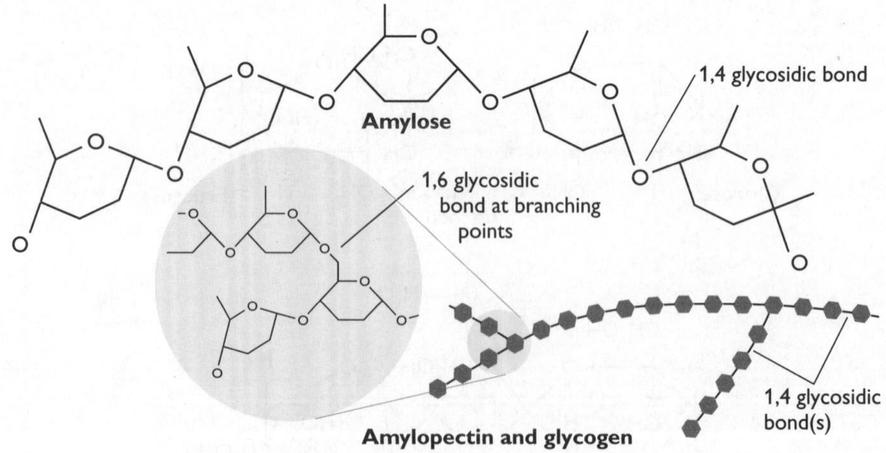

Figure 9 Branching points in amylopectin and glycogen are formed by 1,6 glycosidic bonds

Cellulose is a polymer of β-glucose. Each molecule is a long, straight chain. In cell walls, molecules of cellulose are held together by many hydrogen bonds, forming rigid and tough bundles. These bundles are aligned in cell walls to resist turgor pressure inside plant cells.

The properties of four polysaccharides are summarised in Table 2.

Table 2 Main features of four polysaccharides

Polysaccharide	Monomer	Glycosidic bond(s)	Where found	Functions
Amylose	α-glucose	1,4 (unbranched helical molecule)	Starch grains in chloroplasts and amyloplasts in plants	Energy store in plants
Amylopectin	α-glucose	1,4; 1,6 (branched molecule)	Starch grains in chloroplasts and amyloplasts in plants	Energy store in plants
Glycogen	α-glucose	1,4; 1,6 (branched molecule)	Granules in animal cells, e.g. liver and muscle	Energy store in animals
Cellulose	β-glucose	1,4(straight-chain molecule)	Cell walls of plants	Structural — making cell walls in plants

Knowledge check 5

State the products of hydrolysis of maltose, sucrose, glycogen, amylopectin, amylose and cellulose.

Links

When enzymes break down sucrose and starch, they catalyse the hydrolysis of glycosidic bonds. This guide shows you how to use iodine in the potassium iodide test to follow starch hydrolysis. You will learn more about the production of sugars during photosynthesis in Unit F214 in your A2 course. Simple sugar molecules produced inside chloroplasts are transferred to the rest of the cell and used in respiration or used to make sucrose, starch or cellulose. Sucrose may be exported to the rest of the plant in the phloem (see the Unit Guide for Unit F211).

Lipids

Key concepts you must understand

Lipids are macromolecules. They are not polymers as they do not have repeating sub-units.

Key facts you must know

Lipids are a large, diverse group of compounds. Examples include triglycerides (fats and oils), phospholipids, steroids and waxes. Lipids are not soluble in water; they are soluble in organic solvents.

Like carbohydrates, lipids are composed of carbon, hydrogen and oxygen, but these elements are in different proportions. In lipids, there is far more hydrogen than oxygen. The major components of triglycerides (fats and oils) and phospholipids are fatty acids that have long hydrocarbon chains (Figure 10). The other main component is glycerol.

Examiner tip

A double bond is a covalent bond in which four electrons are shared between atoms rather than the two shared in a single bond. A double bond is stronger than a single bond.

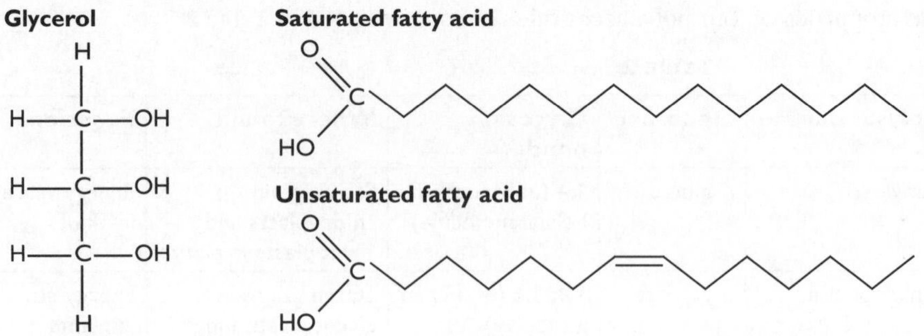

Figure 10 Saturated fatty acids have no double bonds between the carbon atoms, while unsaturated fatty acids have one or more double bonds

Triglycerides

The fatty acids in a triglyceride can be the same as, or different from, each other. The bond that forms between a fatty acid and glycerol is an ester bond. During the formation of an ester bond, water is eliminated — another example of a condensation reaction. Triglyceride structure is shown in Figure 11.

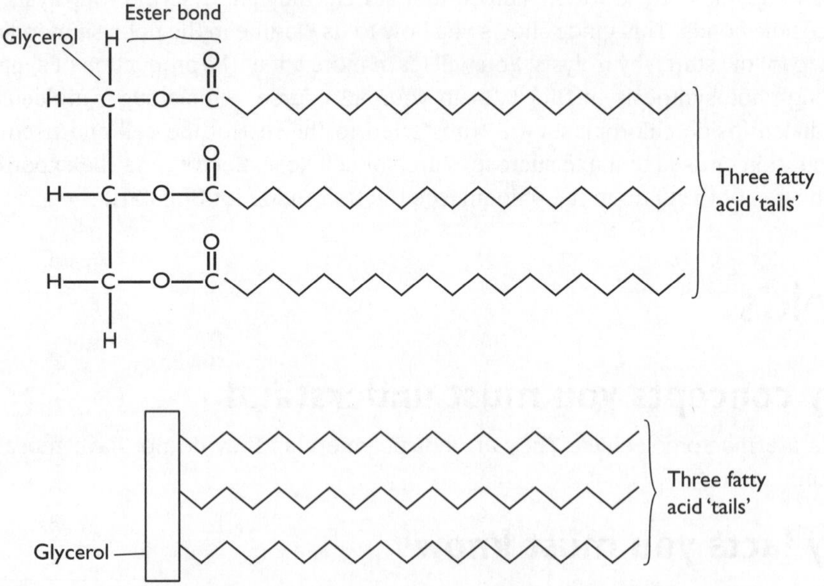

Figure 11 Two ways of showing a triglyceride molecule

Knowledge check 6

Triglycerides and glycogen are used for energy storage. State three ways in which the structure of a triglyceride differs from that of glycogen.

Triglycerides are not soluble in water. They are energy-rich and are therefore excellent for energy storage. When respired, the molecule is oxidised, releasing energy and hydrogen atoms, which form water with oxygen. This is metabolic water, which is important for desert animals, such as gerbils and camels. Fat is less dense than water, and so gives buoyancy to aquatic mammals, such as dolphins and whales. It is also a poor conductor of heat, so is an excellent thermal insulator. Its soft, cushioning effect makes it good for protecting organs, such as the kidneys.

Phospholipids

Phospholipids have a phosphate group attached to glycerol as well as two fatty acids (Figure 12). In most phospholipids the phosphate is attached to nitrogen-containing, water-soluble groups. One of these is choline. This makes the 'head' of the molecule 'water loving' or **hydrophilic**. The two fatty acid chains do not 'like' water: they are **hydrophobic**.

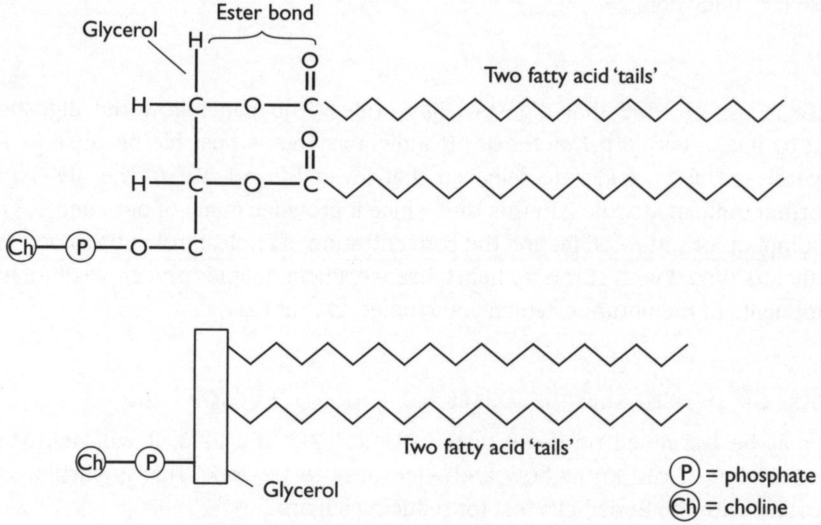

Figure 12 Two ways of showing a phospholipid molecule

Phospholipids form two layers (bilayers) to make membranes. They are ideal for this, as the hydrophilic regions interact with water in the cytoplasm and in fluid outside the cell, while the fatty acid chains form a hydrophobic core. This makes a barrier to the movement of substances in and out of cells as well as organelles made of membranes, such as mitochondria, lysosomes, chloroplasts and endoplasmic reticulum.

Examiner tip
The polar regions of phospholipids form hydrogen bonds with water in fluids outside membranes and cytoplasm inside membranes.

Cholesterol

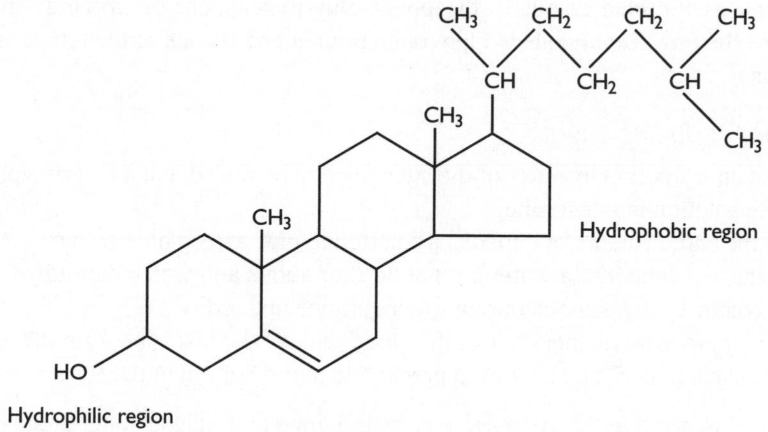

Figure 13 Cholesterol

Examiner tip
The presence or absence of cholesterol in membranes is a key difference between prokaryotes and eukaryotes. See Module 1 of Unit F211 to remind yourself of other differences; this is important in Module 3 of this unit.

Cholesterol (Figure 13) is a lipid-like molecule that is like phospholipids in that it has hydrophobic and hydrophilic regions and is an important component of membranes of eukaryotic cells. It is also used to make steroids, such as testosterone and progesterone. The liver is responsible for metabolising cholesterol for the body. As it is needed everywhere in the body, it has to be transported in the blood, but it is not water soluble so cannot simply dissolve in the blood plasma. There is more about how it is transported to and from the liver in the section on diet and coronary heart disease (see page 36).

Links

Lipase is the enzyme that digests triglycerides. You can follow the digestion of fat by lipase with a pH meter or pH indicator. This is possible because as fat is hydrolysed, fatty acids are released that lower the pH. Fat in the diet is an important topic in Module 2 in this Unit, since it provides much of our energy. The consumption of saturated fat and the concentration of cholesterol in the blood are two factors linked with coronary heart disease. Phospholipids and cholesterol are components of membranes, which you studied in Unit F211.

Knowledge check 7
Explain why ions and polar molecules do not pass through the phospholipid bilayer of cell membranes. How do they pass through these membranes?

Focus on practical skills: tests for biological molecules

You may be examined on these tests in Units F212 and F213. It will help your understanding if you know how and why these tests work. This is particularly important with the Benedict's test for reducing sugars.

Test for starch

- Add a solution of iodine in potassium iodide to a test substance.
- If the iodine solution changes colour from light yellow to blue-black, the test substance contains starch.

Examiner tip
When describing this test, do not write 'iodine'; make sure you give the full name — iodine in potassium iodide solution or simply 'iodine solution'.

The test works because iodine fits inside the helix of the amylose molecules to give the blue colour. All forms of starch in plants contain amylose, but if there is just amylopectin present, then the blue colour does not form and iodine solution is red-brown in colour. Heating a solution of starch with iodine solution in a water bath causes the blue colour to disappear only to reappear on cooling. This is because the amylose uncoils at high temperatures and recoils as the temperature decreases.

Test for reducing sugars

- Make up a solution in water of the substance to be tested. Put a known volume of the solution in a test tube.
- Add the same volume of Benedict's solution to give a deep blue colour.
- Put the test tube into a water bath at 80°C or above and watch carefully to see any colour changes. Look out for green, orange and red.
- When there is no further change in colour, remove the test-tube from the water bath, leave to cool and look for a precipitate at the bottom of the tube.

If the test is positive, you will see a colour change and maybe some precipitate. Remember that this test is not specific to glucose: you will get a positive result with any reducing sugar. The degree of colour change and the quantity of precipitate are determined by the concentration of the reducing sugar. A high reducing sugar concentration gives a red colour and much precipitate. Low concentrations give a hint of a green colour and little, if any, precipitate. Sucrose solution gives a negative result. There is no colour change because sucrose is a **non-reducing sugar**.

Explanation of the Benedict's test

Reducing sugars act as reducing agents because they donate electrons. The electrons are donated by aldehyde or ketone groups that are present in reducing sugars and are exposed when the molecules change from ring structures (see Figure 6, page 13) into straight chain molecules. This happens much more often when the reducing sugar solution is heated. Benedict's solution is made by dissolving copper sulfate in an alkaline solution. The copper ions (Cu^{2+}) give it a blue colour. When heated with a reducing sugar, such as glucose, the Cu^{2+} ions are reduced to Cu^{+}. A further reaction forms red copper oxide, which is insoluble and precipitates. If Benedict's solution is in excess, then the final colour is related to the glucose (or other reducing sugar) concentration. However, at best it is only possible to say that there is a low, medium or high concentration of reducing sugar depending on the final colour.

Examiner tip

As it is not possible to estimate an actual concentration, this method gives **qualitative** results.

Test for non-reducing sugars

You must first test your substance with Benedict's solution (see above) to find out if reducing sugar is present. If the result is negative, then you can carry out the rest of the test. Here is the full procedure:

- Divide a solution of the test substance into two samples (1 and 2).
- Add Benedict's solution to sample 1 and put it in a water bath at 80°C or above.
- If there is no colour change, add a few drops of dilute hydrochloric acid to sample 2 and boil for a few minutes.
- Cool and neutralise with sodium hydrogencarbonate or sodium hydroxide solution.
- Add Benedict's solution and boil; if there is a colour change, the test substance contains a non-reducing sugar.

Examiner tip

Hydrochloric acid catalyses the hydrolysis of the glycosidic bond. When broken, the two monosaccharides are released into the solution.

Sucrose is not a reducing sugar — it cannot donate electrons as it cannot open out into a straight-chain form even when heated. It is a disaccharide made by plants and the glycosidic bond is formed between the groups that would donate electrons. When sucrose is boiled with hydrochloric acid, sucrose molecules are hydrolysed to give glucose and fructose molecules. Glucose and fructose are reducing sugars, which give a positive result when tested with Benedict's solution.

It is possible to make the Benedict's test a **semi-quantitative test** so that you can determine the concentration of reducing sugars in a sample, for example a solution prepared from some plant material. You can do this by making different concentrations of glucose (e.g. 10%, 5%, 1%, 0.5%, 0.1%, 0.05%) and testing them with Benedict's. You can use the final colours as standards to compare against.

Examiner tip

Using colour standards is a semi-quantitative method because the results are subjective. You have to match the colours by eye and not everyone will get the same result. Results may be given as a range, e.g. 1% to 5%, because the colour cannot be matched exactly to one concentration.

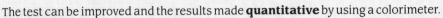

The test can be improved and the results made **quantitative** by using a colorimeter.

- Boil the different concentrations of glucose with Benedict's until there is no further change in colour.
- Cool the tubes and then filter them. Take the filtrates (the liquid that has passed through the filter paper) and test these with a colorimeter that gives a reading for absorbance.
- Plot a graph of absorbance against concentration of glucose. Repeat the procedure with a solution made from the sample following exactly the same procedure.
- Use the graph to find the concentration of reducing sugar in the sample by drawing an intercept from the absorbance reading to the concentration of glucose.

Note that the lighter the colour, the more reducing sugar was present in the test substance. This is because it is the copper ions that give Benedict's solution its blue colour. If these are reduced then they form the precipitate and are not in the filtrate. Without copper ions, the solution is no longer blue. It is possible to remove the residue by spinning the tubes in a centrifuge or just leaving to stand rather than relying on filtration.

Emulsion test for lipids

Examiner tip
This is called an 'emulsion test' because the fine dispersion of the minute droplets of a liquid (e.g. oil) in another in which it does not dissolve, or mix (e.g. water), is called an emulsion.

- Add some alcohol to the test substance.
- Shake and allow the mixture to settle.
- Put some water in a test tube and then pour some of the mixture into the water.
- If a milky cloudiness is visible in the water, then the test is positive.

Alcohol helps to disperse tiny droplets of oil throughout the water, so making it opaque.

Biuret test for proteins

- Make up a solution of the test substance.
- Add dilute sodium hydroxide and dilute copper sulfate. You may be given a biuret solution that contains these two chemicals.
- If the test is positive, a purple or lilac colour appears. If the solution is blue, there is no protein present.

Examiner tip
There is more about the Benedict's test in the Unit Guide to F213/F216 (see examples 4 and 10).

You can make this a semi-quantitative test by making up a series of colour standards with different concentrations of a protein such as albumen. Add biuret solution to give a range of colours. Compare the colour of a test substance with them and estimate which is the closest match. Using a colorimeter, you can make this a quantitative test in the same way as for reducing sugars.

Knowledge check 8
Draw a table to summarise carrying out the tests for biological molecules. Include both positive and negative results in your table.

These tests could be the basis of the qualitative task, the quantitative task and the evaluative task in Unit F213. You are most likely to use the semi-quantitative method, using colour standards for the Benedict's test or for the biuret test. When asked to evaluate, you can always say that more accurate results could be obtained by using a colorimeter. It is always a good idea to have quite a few solutions of known concentration near the likely concentration of the sample to be more confident about where to draw the line on your graph.

Summary

- Water molecules are dipolar and are attracted to each other by hydrogen bonds. This makes water a liquid over a wide range of temperatures and gives water particular properties that contribute to its roles in living organisms.
- Amino acids are the monomers of proteins. A peptide bond is formed by a condensation reaction between the amine group of one amino acid and the carboxylic acid group of another. The products of such condensation reactions are dipeptides and polypeptides. The sequence of amino acids in a polypeptide is the primary structure.
- The secondary structure (α-helix or β-pleated sheet) is the result of folding a polypeptide. Further folding into complex shapes is the tertiary structure. Proteins with more than one polypeptide have quaternary structure.
- Proteins are stabilised by intramolecular hydrogen bonds, ionic bonds and disulfide bridges, and also by hydrophobic and hydrophilic interactions. Hydrogen bonds and ionic bonds break when proteins are heated to high temperatures or are in extremes of pH.
- Haemoglobin is a globular protein that consists of four polypeptide chains that transport oxygen and carbon dioxide. Collagen is a fibrous protein that consists of molecules composed of three helices wound round each other. These are arranged into bundles that give strength to structures such as tendons, ligaments and muscles.
- Monosaccharides are carbohydrates with three to seven carbon atoms. Glucose is a hexose sugar (six carbon atoms). In α-glucose the –H is above the –OH on carbon 1. Starch and glycogen are polymers of α-glucose. In β-glucose the –H is below the –OH on carbon 1. Cellulose is a polymer of β-glucose.
- Glycosidic bonds form between monosaccharides: 1,4 bonds give straight chains; 1,6 bonds give branching points in amylopectin and glycogen.
- Starch (amylose) and cellulose are straight-chain polysaccharides. Amylose has a helical shape and is used as an energy store. Cellulose molecules form hydrogen bonds with adjacent molecules to form strong microfibrils in cell walls. This enables the walls to withstand the turgor pressures inside plant cells.
- A triglyceride is formed from glycerol and three fatty acids. A phospholipid has one fatty acid replaced by phosphate often linked to another water-soluble group, such as choline.
- Triglycerides are insoluble in water and are used for long-term storage of energy. Their high hydrogen content gives high energy release when they are respired. Phospholipids have hydrophilic and hydrophobic regions which results in the formation of bilayers in cell membranes; cholesterol molecules stabilise phospholipid bilayers in membranes of eukaryotic cells.
- Chemical tests are used to identify biological molecules. Starch is identified using iodine solution; reducing and non-reducing sugars using Benedict's solution; proteins with biuret solution; lipids are identified by dissolving in ethanol and adding the solution to water to form an emulsion.
- Water is used in hydrolysis reactions to break down polymers and lipids to their constituent sub-unit molecules.

Nucleic acids

Key concepts you must understand

Nucleic acids are for information storage and retrieval. DNA (deoxyribonucleic acid) is a large, stable molecule found in chromosomes. It forms the genes that code for proteins. You inherited it from your parents and you will pass it on to your children. It is a long-term store of genetic information. RNA (ribonucleic acid) is a shorter molecule that cells use to retrieve information from DNA and express it in the form of proteins. Genes are lengths of nucleotides with a specific sequence of bases. A gene determines the sequence of amino acids in a polypeptide, coding for the order in which amino acids are put together. In DNA there are four bases (A, T, C and G) which cells read in groups of three. These triplets of bases code for the 20 different types of amino acid used to make proteins.

Key facts you must know

DNA and RNA are macromolecules made of repeating sub-units, which are joined together by covalent bonds. Nucleotides are the sub-unit molecules of nucleic acids (Figure 14). Cells join these nucleotides together by forming phosphodiester bonds to make polynucleotides.

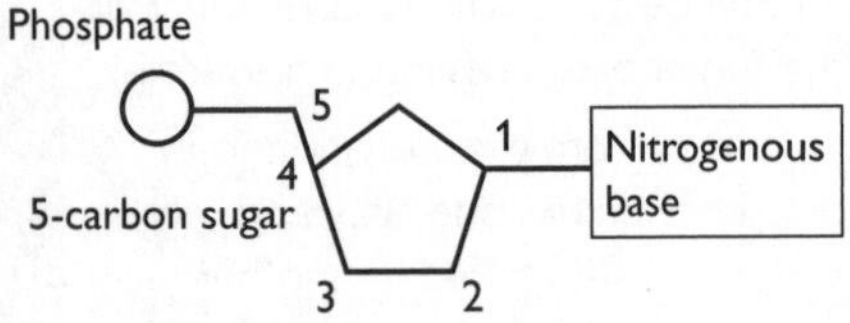

Figure 14 All nucleotides have this structure (the box represents one of five different nitrogenous bases, as in Table 3). The numbers indicate the positions of carbon atoms in the 5-carbon sugar.

The nucleotides that make up DNA contain the sugar deoxyribose; the nucleotides that make up RNA contain ribose. These sugars are pentoses as they have five carbon atoms. There are two types of nitrogenous base: purines and pyrimidines (see Table 3). Purine bases have two rings of carbon and nitrogen atoms; pyrimidines have one.

Table 3 The nitrogenous bases in DNA and RNA

	Purines		Pyrimidines		
Number of rings	2		1		
Bases	Adenine	Guanine	Cytosine	Thymine	Uracil
DNA	✓	✓	✓	✓	✗
RNA	✓	✓	✓	✗	✓

In both DNA and RNA, there are four different bases, but thymine is found only in DNA and uracil is found only in RNA (i.e. in RNA, uracil replaces thymine).

Figure 15 The molecular structure of DNA, showing the two antiparallel polynucleotides

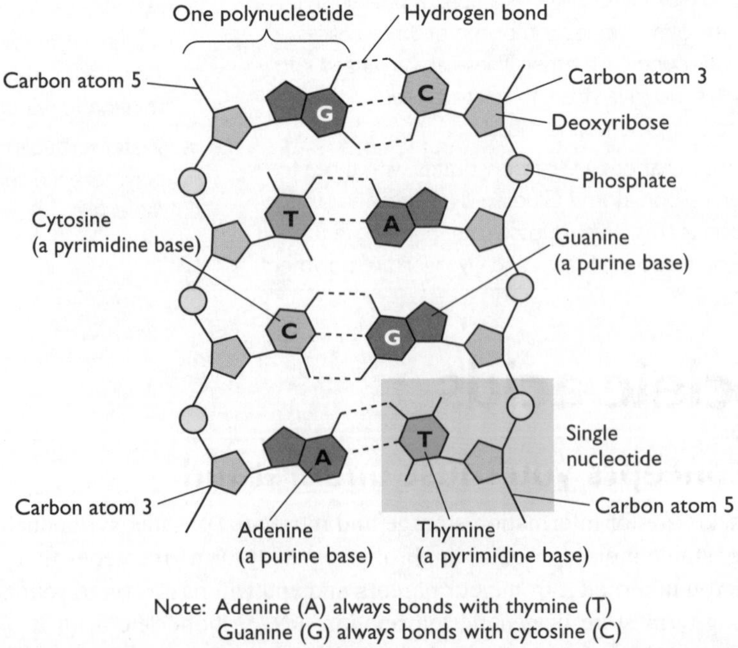

All DNA (except some in viruses) is 'double-stranded'. This means that there are two polynucleotides, or 'strands', side by side. The bases on opposite strands are joined

together by hydrogen bonds (Figure 15). These are not as strong as the covalent bonds joining adjacent nucleotides, but because there are so many it is quite difficult to break the strands apart. This helps to make DNA a stable molecule.

The DNA double helix is shown in Figure 16.

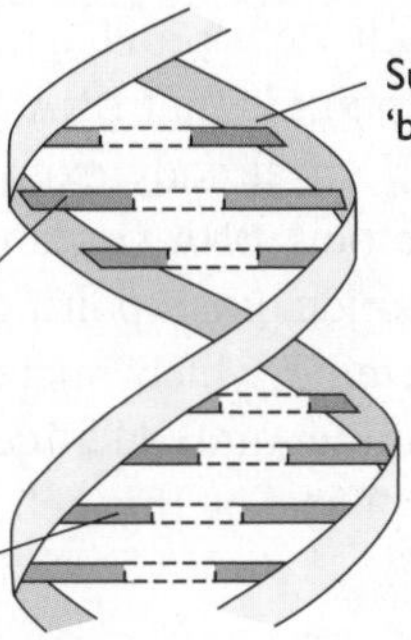

Figure 16 The two 'strands' are twisted around each other to form the DNA double helix (this shows a small part of the double helix of DNA)

Base pairing in DNA is always as follows:

- adenine to thymine (A–T)
- guanine to cytosine (G–C)

Table 4 The three types of RNA

Type of RNA	Function
Messenger RNA (mRNA)	Takes copies of genes from DNA in nucleus to ribosomes
Ribosomal RNA (rRNA)	Helps make sites in ribosomes for assembling proteins from amino acids
Transfer RNA (tRNA)	Carries amino acids to ribosomes

Molecules of RNA are 'single-stranded' polynucleotides. There are hydrogen bonds between some base pairs in tRNA to give a 'cloverleaf' shape. There are no hydrogen bonds in mRNA: it is a single, unfolded chain. The three types of RNA are summarised in Table 4.

DNA and mRNA are compared in Table 5.

Knowledge check 9

State three ways in which the structure of DNA differs from the structure of mRNA.

Table 5 Comparing DNA and messenger RNA

Feature	DNA	Messenger RNA
Overall structure	Double helix	Single chain
Overall size of molecule	Very large	Small
Number of polynucleotide chains	2	1
Name of pentose (5C) sugar	Deoxyribose	Ribose
Nitrogenous bases	Adenine (A), thymine (T), cytosine (C) and guanine (G)	Adenine (A), uracil (U), cytosine (C) and guanine (G)
Base pairing	A pairs with T (A–T) C pairs with G (C–G)	No base pairing
Function	Long-term storage of genetic information	Transfer of genetic information from nucleus to ribosomes
Where found in eukaryotic cells	Nucleus (also some in mitochondria and chloroplasts)	Nucleus and cytoplasm; also attached to ribosomes when protein is being made

Replication

Key concepts you must understand

Examiner tip
Conservative replication would produce DNA molecules with two newly synthesised polynucleotides, rather than one old and one new as in semi-conservative replication.

DNA replication is DNA copying itself. Cells provide nucleotides, energy and enzymes for the process, but the important point is that DNA acts as a **template** so that new polynucleotide chains are built up on already existing ones. This is called **semi-conservative replication**, as the new DNA contains one 'old' polynucleotide (the template) and one 'new' polynucleotide. Base-pairing is important because exposed bases on the template DNA determine which nucleotide is next in the sequence. Cytosine always pairs with guanine and adenine always pairs with thymine. Replication happens during interphase of the cell cycle (see the Unit Guide for Unit F211).

Key facts you must know

Think of replication as a series of events with a beginning, a middle and an end.

- DNA unwinds and hydrogen bonds holding the bases together are broken.
- Polynucleotide chains separate, exposing bases along both polynucleotide chains.
- Each chain acts as a template so a new chain can be built up, following the rules of base pairing — A–T and C–G.
- Free nucleotide molecules in the nucleus are put in position alongside the exposed bases — each nucleotide consists of a pentose sugar, base and three phosphates.
- As the nucleotides 'line up', they form a growing chain.
- Two of the phosphates from each nucleotide break off in a reaction that forms a covalent bond between the new nucleotide and the growing chain.
- DNA polymerase (an enzyme) joins the nucleotides in the correct sequence.
- DNA polymerase checks the new base sequence to make sure it is correct. It acts to proof-read the new polynucleotide. If there is an incorrect nucleotide, it cuts it out and replaces it.
- Hydrogen bonds form between the bases on opposite polynucleotide chains — the template chain and the newly synthesised chain.
- DNA winds up again into a double helix. Replication is complete.

Knowledge check 10
Both polynucleotides act as templates during DNA replication. Explain the term *template* in this context.

DNA replication is illustrated in Figure 17.

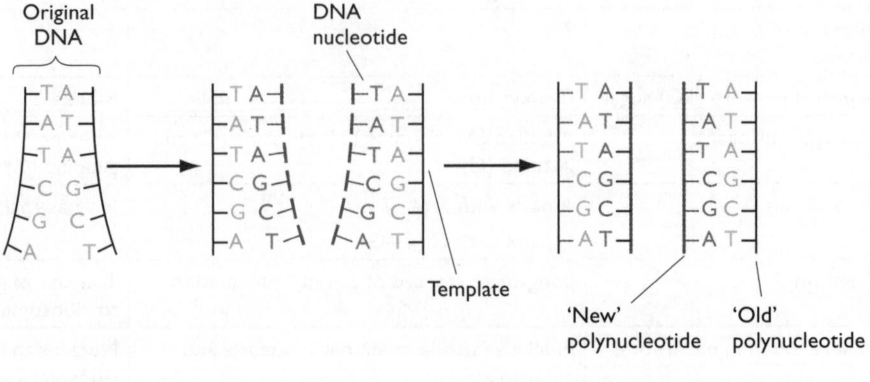

Figure 17 The stages of DNA replication shown in a very simple fashion

Links

You only need to know an outline of protein synthesis for this Unit. You will cover the topic again in more detail in Unit F215 at A2. For Unit F211 you need to know how the nucleus, rough endoplasmic reticulum, Golgi apparatus and secretory vesicles are involved in protein synthesis (see the Unit Guide for Unit F211). Decoding the human and other genomes has involved 'reading' sequences of bases throughout DNA. The way in which genomes are sequenced is also covered in Unit F215.

Summary

- Nucleic acids (RNA and DNA) are polymers of nucleotides. Each nucleotide consists of a pentose sugar, phosphate and a base. Genetic information is stored as DNA and retrieved in the form of RNA during protein synthesis.
- DNA is a polynucleotide that is usually double-stranded. The nucleotides contain deoxyribose, phosphate, the purine bases adenine (A) and guanine (G), and the pyrimidine bases thymine (T) and cytosine (C).
- Hydrogen bonding between A and T and between G and C holds the two polynucleotides of DNA together. The polynucleotides are antiparallel with carbons 3 and 5 of deoxyribose facing in opposite directions giving a double helix with one strand running in the 3′ to 5′ direction and the other in the 5′ to 3′ direction.
- RNA is a polynucleotide that is usually single-stranded. The nucleotides contain the bases A, G, C and uracil (U). There are three forms of RNA: messenger RNA, transfer RNA and ribosomal RNA.
- In semi-conservative replication, each polynucleotide of DNA acts as a template for the assembly of a new polynucleotide by DNA polymerase. The enzyme corrects mistakes in base pairing between nucleotides and the template polynucleotide.
- A gene is a sequence of bases in DNA that codes for the assembly of amino acids to give the primary structure of a polypeptide.

Enzymes

Key concepts you must understand

Enzymes are proteins that catalyse chemical reactions. Without enzymes, these reactions would occur too slowly to support life as we know it. Reactions occur when molecules collide. Enzymes provide a place where reactions are likely to occur because they hold molecules under a strain, causing bonds to break and/or form. When molecules collide with enzymes in this way, they are described as successful collisions.

Knowledge check 11

Enzymes are biological catalysts. Explain what this means.

Key facts you must know

Enzymes:

- provide a site where molecules are brought together, so that reactions occur more easily than elsewhere
- remain unchanged at the end of a reaction
- catalyse reactions in which compounds are built up
- catalyse reactions in which compounds are broken down
- change substrate molecules into product molecules

- **intracellular enzymes** work inside cells; examples are catalase and the enzymes of respiration and photosynthesis
- **extracellular enzymes** work outside cells; examples are amylase and lipase, which are secreted into the small intestine

Enzymes are globular proteins with a tertiary structure held together by intramolecular bonds (see Figure 5). Different enzymes have different 3D shapes.

How enzymes work

The **active site** is the part of an enzyme where reactions occur. It is a cleft or depression on the surface of the molecule — a shape that fits around the substrate molecule. Therefore, enzymes and their substrates fit together like a **lock and key** to form an **enzyme–substrate complex**. When the reaction is over, the product (or products) leaves so that another substrate molecule can enter the active site (see Figure 18).

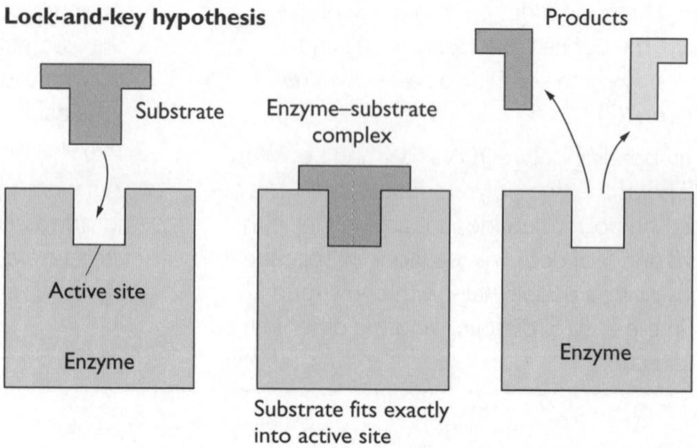

Figure 18 The lock-and-key mechanism of enzyme action

'Lock-and-key' is a simple model. There is evidence to show that the **induced-fit** model (Figure 19), in which the enzyme's active site moulds around the substrate, is a more likely mechanism.

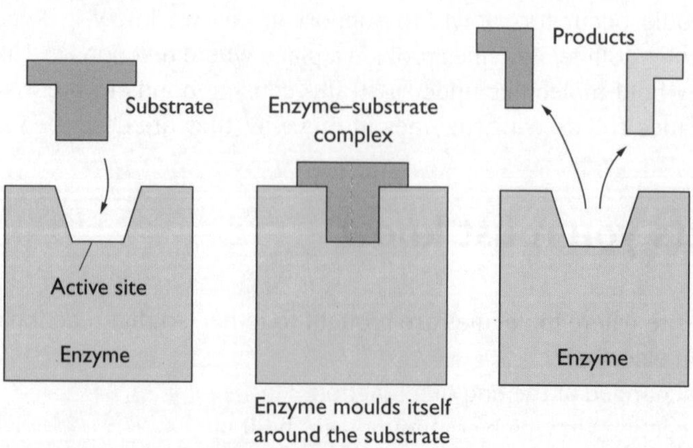

Figure 19 The induced-fit mechanism of enzyme action

Each enzyme has a specific shape and usually only one type of substrate molecule fits the active site. Note that the substrate is *not* the same shape as the active site. It has a shape that fits into the active site, i.e. the two are **complementary**. Some enzymes are not as **specific** as others, having active sites that will accept a variety of substrate molecules with similar shapes.

Activation energy is the energy needed to break chemical bonds in reacting molecules. The reactions involved in breaking and making strong covalent bonds occur extremely slowly without enzymes because there is not enough energy to change substrate molecules to product molecules. Enzymes lower activation energy by providing active sites where reactions occur much more easily. The idea of activation energy is shown by the graph in Figure 20.

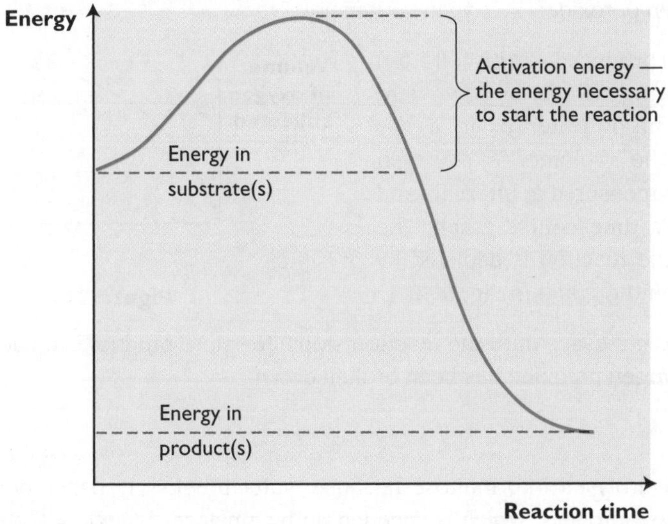

Figure 20 A graph showing the idea of activation energy

Enzyme molecules have specific shapes determined by their tertiary structure. Some enzymes have a quaternary structure as well, since their molecules comprise two or more polypeptides. This means that some enzyme molecules have more than one active site. Each molecule of catalase has four identical polypeptides and therefore has four active sites.

The tertiary structure of enzymes is altered by changes in pH and increases in temperature. As a result, active sites change shape and no longer accept substrate molecules.

Links

Many practical investigations involve enzymes. You need to have an understanding of what enzymes are and how they function to explain what happens in these experiments. Note that the active site is complementary in shape to the substrate. Other examples of this 'fitting together' are:

- antigens and antibodies
- antigens and receptors on the surfaces of T and B lymphocytes
- hormones and their receptors
- neurotransmitters and their receptors at synapses

Examiner tip

Complementary (*not* complimentary) refers to the matching shapes of an enzyme's active site and the substrate molecule that fits into it. **Specificity** applies to enzymes that act on one substrate, or a limited range of similar substrate molecules. Use both terms when explaining enzyme action.

Knowledge check 12

Explain why enzymes are made from polypeptides and not from polysaccharides.

Focus on practical skills: following an enzyme-catalysed reaction

Hydrogen peroxide

Hydrogen peroxide is a toxic substance that is produced in organisms by several reactions. The enzyme **catalase** speeds up the breakdown of hydrogen peroxide to water and oxygen. Catalase is found in all sorts of things, from blood to sticks of celery.

This is the reaction that occurs:

$$2H_2O_2 \rightarrow O_2 + 2H_2O$$

hydrogen peroxide → oxygen + water

The oxygen produced can be collected in a measuring cylinder by downward displacement of water or in a gas syringe. The volume of oxygen collected is measured at intervals and plotted on a time–course graph. The course of the reaction is depicted by the curve on the graph in Figure 21.

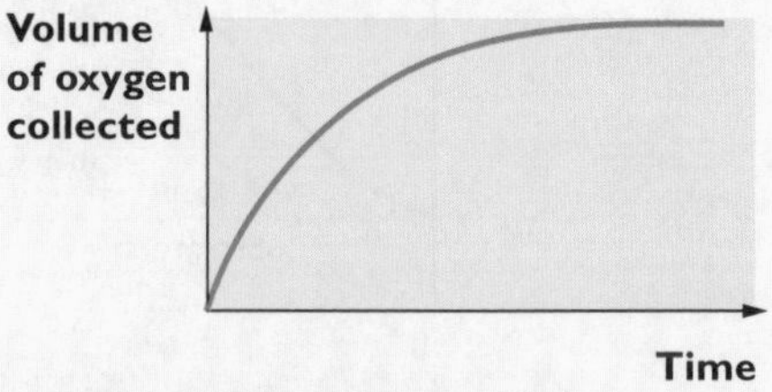

Figure 21

The volume increases until the reaction stops. No more product is made because all the hydrogen peroxide has been broken down.

Starch

Starch is hydrolysed into maltose because water breaks glycosidic bonds. This is a very slow process, which is speeded up by amylase. To follow the course of the reaction, some amylase is added to a starch solution and samples from the reaction mixture are tested with iodine solution. At the beginning, the colour is blue-black. As the reaction proceeds, there is less and less starch and so the colour is lighter. Eventually, there is no colour change to the iodine solution. At this point, the reaction is complete — all the starch has been changed into maltose.

The course of starch hydrolysis is shown by the graph in Figure 22.

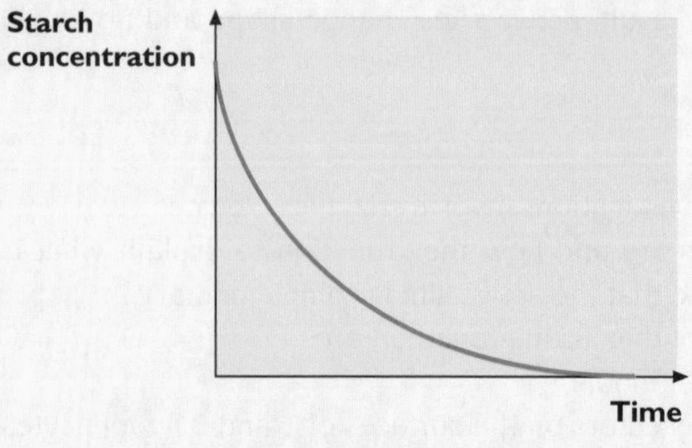

Figure 22

Time–course graphs

The rate of these reactions changes with time. They are at their fastest to begin with, when there is the maximum concentration of substrate. They are at their slowest towards the end, when almost all of the substrate has been changed into product. When all the substrate has been used up, the reaction stops.

Rates of enzyme-catalysed reactions are determined by collisions between substrate and enzyme molecules. At the beginning, there are many collisions; later, there are fewer and fewer. The rate slows down because there is less and less substrate. The quantity of enzyme stays the same, but as time progresses there is less substrate to fit into the active sites available. The concentration of substrate begins to limit the reaction. The **turnover number** for an enzyme is the maximum number of substrate molecules that fit into the active site in a unit of time.

Links

To investigate the effect of factors such as temperature and pH on enzyme activity, a number of time–course experiments need to be carried out and the rate of reaction found for each. The results are then plotted on a graph to show the effect of the factor investigated. Enzyme activity is often measured by finding the rate of reaction at the beginning of the time–course graph. This is called the initial rate. You can find this by drawing a tangent on the graph. For more information see Question 3, page 77 and examples 5 and 14–18 in the Unit Guide for F213/F216.

Enzyme activity

Key concepts you must understand

Enzymes are globular proteins that catalyse metabolic reactions. The active site is formed by folding of the protein (tertiary structure). Denaturation is the loss of shape of the active site when intramolecular bonds break at high temperature. Changes in pH may also cause them to break. Rates of reaction are influenced by the initial concentration of substrate and by the concentration of enzymes. Many enzymes require cofactors in order to work. Inhibitors fit into enzyme molecules, preventing them from working.

Examiner tip

Metabolism is the sum of chemical and physical changes that occur in an organism. Enzymes catalyse reactions that (a) break down substrate molecules to smaller products (e.g. breakdown of hydrogen peroxide) and (b) build up (synthesise) larger product molecules from smaller substrate molecules (e.g. DNA from nucleotides).

Key facts you must know

Temperature

Separate test tubes of starch solution and amylase solution are placed in a water bath at 10°C and left to reach this temperature; then the two are mixed together. Samples are taken at intervals from the reaction mixture and tested with iodine solution, until there is no colour change. The time taken for the reaction to finish can be converted into a rate by calculating 1/(time taken). This is then repeated for more temperatures (e.g. 0, 20, 30, 40, 50 and 60°C), and the results plotted on a graph (see Figure 23). You

Examiner tip

Equilibration is the term used to describe leaving separate tubes of solutions of substrate and enzyme to reach the desired temperature.

can also follow the reaction using a colorimeter. Samples taken at the beginning of the reaction are dark blue and give a high reading for absorbance. Samples taken at the end of the reaction are light yellow and give a low reading. The initial rate may be calculated by drawing a graph of absorbance readings against time and taking a tangent. It is better to take the absorbance readings of known concentrations of starch and iodine solution and draw a calibration curve (absorbance plotted against concentration of starch). The calibration curve allows you to convert absorbance readings taken as the reaction proceeds into concentrations of starch.

Note that you cannot add iodine solution to the reaction mixture and watch it gradually change colour because iodine inhibits amylase.

Examiner tip
Enzyme activity is sometimes used as the *y*-axis label instead of rate of reaction.

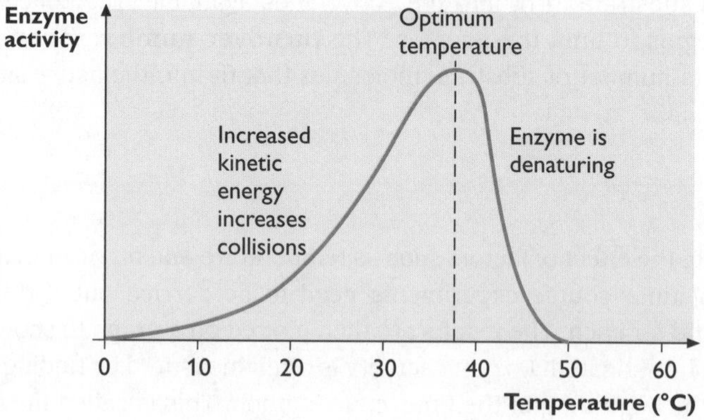

Figure 23 The effect of temperature on the rate of an enzyme-catalysed reaction

Examiner tip
Not all enzymes behave like this. Enzymes from organisms that live in very cold habitats have optimum temperatures much lower than 37°C. Enzymes from bacteria that live in hot springs are active at temperatures up to 90°C.

This is a *description* of the effect of temperature, as shown in Figure 23:
- Enzymes show no activity at freezing temperatures.
- Their activity increases as they are warmed from freezing.
- They are most active at their optimum temperature (human enzymes 37°C).
- They are less active at temperatures below and above the optimum.
- There is no activity at high temperatures (e.g. above 50°C).

This is an *explanation* of these effects:
- At freezing temperatures there is no molecular movement, so no collisions occur.
- Enzymes are not denatured by freezing as they function on warming up.
- As temperature increases, substrate and enzyme molecules have more kinetic energy, so there are more successful collisions between substrate molecules and enzyme molecules.
- At high temperatures, there is excessive movement within the enzyme molecules so bonds (e.g. ionic and hydrogen) break, the active site changes shape and no longer accepts the substrate — the enzyme molecules are denatured.

pH

An investigation similar to the one described for temperature can be carried out for pH using different buffer solutions with the reaction mixtures. Buffer solutions maintain a constant pH. There are different buffer solutions available to give a range from pH 3 to pH 11. The results of such an experiment are shown in the graph in Figure 24.

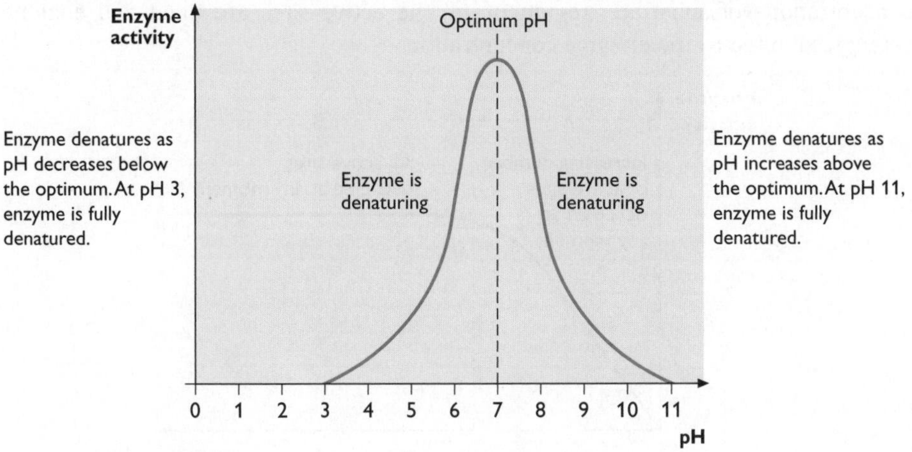

Figure 24 The effect of pH on an enzyme-catalysed reaction

This is a *description* of the effects of pH, as shown in Figure 24:

- The enzyme is most active at a certain pH — the optimum pH.
- It is less active either side of the optimum pH.
- It is inactive at extremes of pH.

This is an *explanation* of these effects:

- pH is a measure of hydrogen ion concentration; as the pH of a solution changes, the charges on the R groups of amino acids change.
- At low pH, when the concentration of hydrogen ions is high, many of these ions interact with negatively charged R groups, so cancelling out their charge.
- This disrupts the ionic bonding between oppositely charged R groups within the tertiary structure — the enzyme shape changes.
- When active sites change shape, they no longer have shapes complementary to their substrates and cannot form enzyme–substrate complexes.
- At a high pH there is a low concentration of hydrogen ions and positively charged R groups lose hydrogen ions to the surrounding solution. This means that these R groups lose their charge so that ionic bonds break. The tertiary structure is distorted, changing the shape of the active site.
- The interaction between substrate molecules and active sites often depends on the charges on R groups. Changes in pH therefore make it less likely that substrate molecules will be held in place within active sites.

Examiner tip

pH is not a simple linear scale. A change of one pH unit (e.g. pH 7.0 to pH 8.0) represents a change in concentration of hydrogen ions by a factor of 10.

Examiner tip

When describing graphs like those in this section, make sure you use words such as increase, decrease, peak, maximum, minimum, constant and plateau. It is often a good idea to rule lines on graphs to divide them into sections and then write about each section.

Substrate concentration

The effect of substrate concentration is investigated by setting up a series of test tubes, all with the same concentration of enzyme, but with different concentrations of substrate. The initial rate of reaction in each tube is determined and plotted on a graph (see Figure 25). Note that on Figure 25 the plotted points have not been included, just a smooth curve.

The **limiting factor** of enzyme activity is the one that restricts that activity. As the concentration of substrate is increased, the rate of reaction increases (see region A on the curve) because there are more substrate molecules for the enzymes to act on. Substrate concentration is the factor that **limits** the rate of reaction. At high concentrations of substrate (region B), all the active sites are filled and enzyme activity is limited by the enzyme concentration.

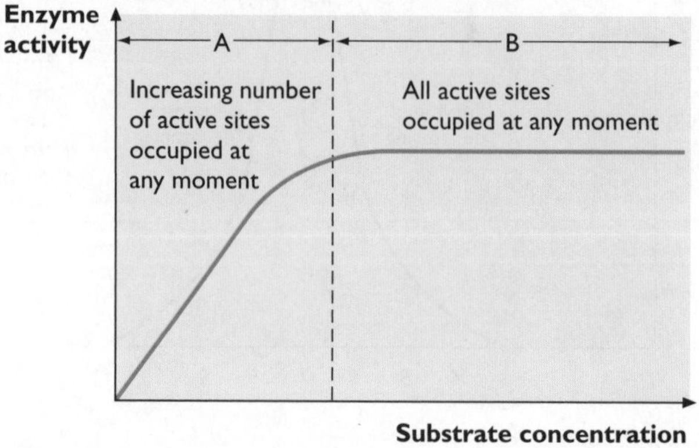

Figure 25 The effect of substrate concentration on enzyme activity

Examiner tip

Use the words **limiting factor** when writing about enzyme activity. You can explain the enzyme activity in these graphs in terms of the factor(s) that limit the activity or do not limit it.

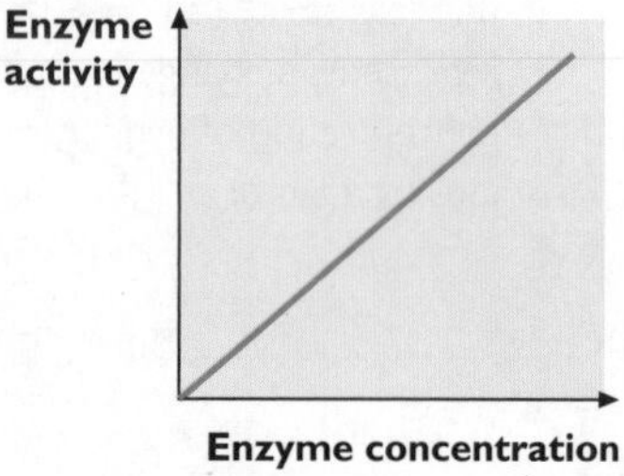

Figure 26 The effect of enzyme concentration on enzyme activity

Enzyme concentration

The investigation is repeated with the substrate concentration kept constant and the enzyme concentration increased. The result is as shown in Figure 26.

With more enzyme molecules, there are more active sites available and so the only limiting factor is the enzyme concentration. This happens if there is an excess of substrate at each enzyme concentration tested.

Cofactors and coenzymes

Some enzymes do not function unless they are combined with a cofactor. Cofactors may be ions or complex organic substances, which may occupy the active site and take part in the reaction or are involved in other ways. Coenzymes are organic cofactors that are changed slightly during the reaction catalysed by the enzyme. Most coenzymes are mobile and travel back and forth between enzymes. The roles of some cofactors and coenzymes are given in Table 6.

Table 6 Cofactors and coenzymes

Enzyme	**Cofactor**	**Role of enzyme**
Urease	Nickel (Ni^{2+})	Hydrolyses urea to ammonia and carbon dioxide
Carbonic anhydrase	Zinc (Zn^{2+})	Involved in transport of carbon dioxide in the blood
Catalase	Haem (containing iron as Fe^{2+})	Breaks down hydrogen peroxide
Enzyme(s)	**Coenzyme**	**Role of coenzyme**
Several enzymes in photosynthesis	NADP	Transfer of hydrogen from water to carbon dioxide in photosynthesis
Several enzymes in respiration	NAD and FAD	Transfer of hydrogen during respiration
Pyruvate dehydrogenase (a mitochondrial enzyme)	Coenzyme A	Transfers acetyl groups (C_2H_3O) from pyruvate and fatty acids during respiration

Inhibitors

Inhibitors slow down enzyme-catalysed reactions by fitting into sites on the enzyme.

Competitive inhibitors:

- fit into the active site
- have a shape similar to, but not the same as, the substrate
- block the substrate from entering the active site
- prevent the formation of enzyme–substrate complexes
- have an effect that can be reversed by increasing the concentration of substrate

The mode of action of a competitive inhibitor is shown in Figure 27.

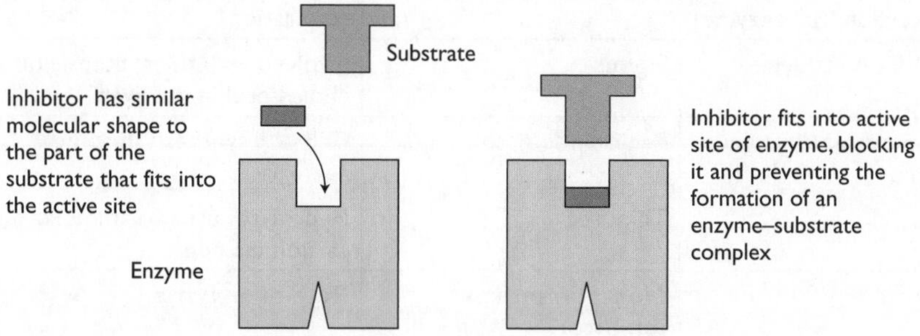

Figure 27 Competitive inhibitors fit into the active site and block it

Non-competitive inhibitors:

- do not fit into the active site
- fit into a site elsewhere on the enzyme
- cause the active site to change shape so it is no longer complementary in shape to the substrate
- have an effect that cannot be reversed by increasing the concentration of substrate

The mode of action of a non-competitive inhibitor is shown in Figure 28.

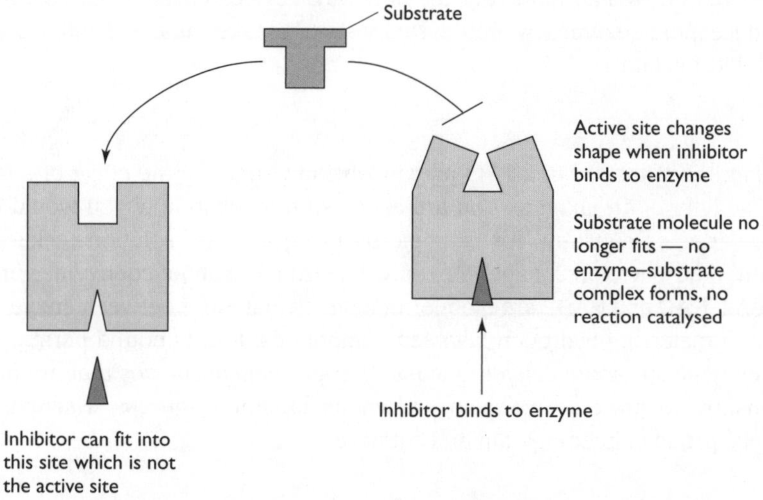

Figure 28 Non-competitive inhibitors fit into another site on the enzyme, leading to a change in the active site

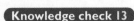

Non-competitive inhibition is used to control multi-step metabolic pathways in cells. Each reaction in a pathway is catalysed by a different enzyme. As the final product accumulates, it inhibits the enzyme at the beginning of the pathway, so slowing down or stopping production. This is called end-product inhibition and is used to ensure that cells do not waste energy and resources making products that are not required.

Knowledge check 13

State the difference between a competitive and a non-competitive enzyme inhibitor.

Some inhibitors and the enzymes they inhibit are given in Table 7.

Table 7 Competitive and non-competitive inhibitors and the enzymes they inhibit

Enzyme	Competitive inhibitor	Role of enzyme
Succinate dehydrogenase (a mitochondrial enzyme)	Malonic acid	Transfers hydrogen during respiration
HMG-CoA reductase	Statins	Involved with the synthesis of cholesterol in the liver
Transpeptidase in some bacteria	Penicillin *	Cell wall synthesis in some bacteria
Urease	Thiourea	Hydrolyses urea to ammonia and carbon dioxide
Enzyme	**Non-competitive inhibitor**	**Role of enzyme**
Cytochrome oxidase (a mitochondrial enzyme)	Potassium cyanide, KCN *	Catalyses important step in respiration in mitochondria

Asterisks (*) indicate non-reversible inhibitors. The others are reversible.

Examiner tip

This table may look difficult because of all the long names. It shows you the importance of these inhibitors. Make sure that you learn the principles of enzyme inhibition and can explain them (see the topic summary).

Some inhibitors are reversible and some are non-reversible. Many drugs act on enzymes to inhibit them; examples are penicillin and the statins (see Table 7). Some poisons are enzyme inhibitors. If you see an examination question that tells you that the rate of an enzyme-catalysed reaction slows down following the addition of a substance, then that substance is likely to be an inhibitor. If the effect is reversed by increasing the concentration of substrate, then it is a competitive inhibitor. If enzymes are inhibited permanently, the only way a cell can overcome this inhibition is to produce more enzymes by protein synthesis. This takes time and will not happen if the inhibitor is fatal.

Examiner tip

Take care when answering questions that ask you to 'describe' and 'explain', particularly questions on enzymes. In a describe question, simply translate the pattern or trend you can see in the graph into words using appropriate vocabulary: increase, decrease, peak, constant, etc. When writing an explanation, think of what happens at the molecular level.

Links

The quantitative task in Unit F213 may involve investigating the effect of a factor on the activity of an enzyme. You are expected to explain how you would keep control variables constant, for example by using a buffer solution to keep pH constant. (See Question 3, page 77.) You will learn more about coenzymes in Unit F214 at A2. NAD and NADP are mobile coenzymes that move between enzymes in the cell, transferring hydrogen between compounds. FAD is bound permanently to the enzyme succinate dehydrogenase. Non-protein substances that are bound permanently to proteins are also known as prosthetic groups. Haem is the prosthetic group of haemoglobin and catalase.

Summary

- Enzymes are globular proteins that catalyse metabolic reactions involving breakdown of substrate molecules (e.g. hydrogen peroxide) and synthesis of molecules (e.g. DNA). Intracellular enzymes act inside cells; extracellular enzymes act outside cells. e.g. in the gut lumen.
- Activation energy has to be overcome before a reaction can proceed. Enzymes lower activation energy by having active sites where substrate molecules fit, either because they have a complementary shape (lock and key) or because the enzyme moulds around the substrate (induced fit) to form an enzyme–substrate complex.
- Enzymes have different degrees of specificity. Some only accept one type of substrate molecule; less specific enzymes accept several similar substrate molecules.
- Rates of activity are influenced by several factors, including temperature, pH, substrate concentration and enzyme concentration. The effect of each factor is investigated by using five or more reaction mixtures across an appropriate range (e.g. 0°C to 70°C), determining the initial rates of reaction and plotting a graph. The effect of each factor gives a characteristic trend or pattern.
- Cofactors are required for the functioning of enzymes. Ions, such as Zn^{2+}, fit into active sites and take part in the reaction but are not changed like the substrate is. Complex organic compounds that act as cofactors are called coenzymes. Some of these are reduced or oxidised during reactions and transport hydrogen between compounds.
- An inhibitor reduces the activity of an enzyme by either competing with the substrate for the active site (competitive inhibitor) or attaching to another site on the enzyme to alter the shape of the active site (non-competitive inhibitor). Poisons (e.g. cyanide) and medicinal drugs (e.g. penicillin) are enzyme inhibitors. Potassium cyanide inhibits cytochrome oxidase in mitochondria so stopping respiration.

Module 2: Food and health

Diet and food production

Key concepts you must understand

A balanced diet provides macronutrients, micronutrients, water and fibre. Carbohydrates, fats and proteins are the macronutrients that provide energy and the carbon compounds we need to make biochemical molecules that make up our cells, tissues and organs. Vitamins and minerals are micronutrients, as we require them in such small quantities.

An unbalanced diet may lead to malnutrition. Obesity is a form of malnutrition.

Key facts you must know

A balanced diet must provide us with:

- the energy we need
- nutrients for many functions, including making biological molecules in cells:
  - essential amino acids (EAAs)
  - essential fatty acids (EFAs)
  - vitamins
  - minerals

- sufficient water to replace losses
- fibre

Proteins provide amino acids for our cells to make their proteins. We cannot synthesise the eight **essential amino acids** (EAAs) and therefore they have to be present in our diet. Fats similarly provide two fatty acids that we cannot synthesise — they are known as **essential fatty acids** (EFAs). Vitamins are complex organic compounds that we cannot synthesise, so must be in our diet. They have a variety of roles, such as making coenzymes. Minerals are inorganic ions that are used for many functions — for example, calcium and magnesium for making bones and teeth.

Water in the diet replaces what is lost in breath, sweat, etc. It is the solvent in blood plasma, tissue fluid and cytoplasm. It also takes part in hydrolysis reactions during digestion and, as sweat, helps us lose heat to our surroundings.

Fibre contains cellulose that we cannot digest; it helps to prevent constipation and lowers the risks of heart disease and bowel cancer.

Obesity

If a person's body mass is 20% or more above the recommended mass for his/her height, then that person is obese. The energy intake has far exceeded the energy consumption and the excess has been stored as fat. Obese people are at risk from a variety of diseases such as diabetes, arthritis and coronary heart disease. There is more about this in Question 4 (page 83).

Diet and coronary heart disease

Key concepts you must understand

Coronary heart disease (CHD) is a degenerative condition that involves the build-up of fatty tissue in the walls of the arteries that supply the heart muscle. If these arteries become narrowed as a result, the flow of blood decreases and the supply of nutrients and oxygen to the heart muscle are restricted. The muscle does not release enough energy and the heart becomes weak. There may be a blood clot in the coronary artery, so cutting off the supply of blood to that area completely and leading to a heart attack.

Key facts you must know

Lipoproteins are particles made in the liver for movement of cholesterol in the bloodstream. Cholesterol is not water soluble, so has to be packaged in these particles, which are coated with phospholipids and proteins so that they can travel in the blood plasma; the centre contains cholesterol, triglycerides and other lipids. There are two types of lipoprotein:

- low-density lipoproteins (LDL), which take cholesterol to the tissues
- high-density lipoproteins (HDL), which remove cholesterol from tissues and return it to the liver

When spun in a centrifuge, LDLs rise to the top of the tube, HDLs sink towards the bottom. HDLs have a lower proportion of lipid than LDLs.

Knowledge check 14

Explain how lipoproteins transport cholesterol, which is not soluble in water, in blood plasma.

The endothelial lining of blood vessels should be smooth to allow the free flow of blood. High blood pressure may cause lesions (or breaks) in the endothelium of coronary arteries; if this happens then LDLs enter the inner layer of these arteries. The cholesterol and fat they carry is oxidised and builds up in the wall of the arteries forming atheromatous plaque. This enlarges the wall so there is less space for blood to flow. Plaque gives a rough lining to arteries, which increases the chances of blood clots forming, so decreasing the diameter of the lumen even more.

Examiner tip
Endothelium is the single layer of squamous cells that lines all blood vessels. See Module 2 of Unit F211.

Among the factors that influence the development of fatty tissue in the coronary arteries is diet. Diets rich in saturated fat tend to increase the cholesterol concentration of the blood. Polyunsaturated fats in foods such as oily fish tend to have the opposite effect. Individuals concerned about their blood cholesterol are advised to avoid foods rich in saturated fat and cholesterol. Antioxidants, such as vitamins C and E, are protective in that they help to reduce the chances of developing CHD. Fresh fruit and vegetables are rich sources and should be included in the diet. Statins are taken by people with high blood cholesterol to reduce their chance of heart disease.

Examiner tip
People with high blood cholesterol concentrations may take statins. These drugs act as competitive inhibitors of an enzyme involved in cholesterol synthesis (see Table 7).

A stroke occurs when the blood supply in an artery to the brain is interrupted. This may happen because there is a blood clot or because the artery is weakened by plaque and bursts. Blood may leak into the brain tissue, which can be fatal. If not, then certain brain functions (such as speech and memory) may be impaired, either temporarily or permanently.

Links

There are numerous links with Module 1 here. You should look at:

- the structure and functions of carbohydrates, proteins and fats to see why they are important in the diet
- the roles of water
- the role of ions, e.g. iron for making haem for haemoglobin and catalase
- the B vitamins that are used to make coenzymes, e.g. riboflavin for FAD and nicotinic acid for NAD
- cholesterol as an important constituent of membranes (see the Unit Guide for Unit F211)

When studying the link between diet and CHD, it is a good idea to remind yourself of the structure and function of the heart (Unit F211), especially the position and function of the coronary arteries. There is more about cardiovascular diseases in the section on smoking (see page 51).

Feed the world

Key concepts you must understand

You will have studied **food chains** and **trophic levels** at GCSE. Food chains show the flow of energy by using arrows to point from food to feeder. The first organisms in the chain are producers, such as grasses or trees. Producers are **autotrophs**, which use an external energy source and simple inorganic molecules (carbon dioxide and water) and ions, such as nitrate and phosphate, to make complex organic molecules

Examiner tip
Beware of the two uses of the term food chain. In biology, it refers to the flow of energy from producers to consumers with three, four or five organisms in the chain. The human food chain refers to the production, processing, storage and transport of our foodstuffs.

(proteins, carbohydrates, lipids and nucleic acids). Other organisms in food chains are **heterotrophs**, which are organisms that take in complex organic molecules as sources of energy and carbon compounds to use in their metabolism.

Humans have been improving domesticated animals and plants by **artificial selection** since the Neolithic period, about 10 000 years ago. Choosing the animals and plants that will be kept for breeding and then pairing them is selective breeding. Knowledge of genetics has improved this process over the past 100 years.

Key facts you must know

Regardless of what you eat, your diet ultimately depends on plants; they capture light energy in photosynthesis and transfer energy to compounds such as starch, proteins and lipids that they make using carbon dioxide, water and a variety of mineral ions such as nitrate and phosphate. Plants have many more multi-step metabolic processes than us and produce a wide range of compounds.

Many foods in our diet come directly or via processing from plants. Examples are staple foods such as rice, potatoes and maize; also vegetables, fruits, bread and cakes. The energy has been through one trophic level and then comes to us as primary consumers. Domesticated animals, such as cattle and pigs, are primary consumers. When we eat animal products we are a secondary consumer. Sometimes we are tertiary consumers, for example when we eat fish, which often feed as secondary consumers.

Selective breeding

Animal breeding

Examiner tip
Do not confuse selective breeding with genetic engineering. Genetic engineering began in the 1960s and is used to improve domesticated plants and animals, and prokaryotes used in biotechnology. This involves moving individual genes (or groups of genes) between organisms — something that is not possible with selective breeding.

Breeders choose features of their animals that they want to improve. Animals in the herd or flock are chosen for their appearance or productivity: these are selected and bred together. The breeder checks the offspring to see if they show the desired features and any improvement. The best are selected, bred together and the process is continued with future generations. For some species, such as cattle, breeders use sperm from males that have superior qualities. By using artificial insemination, sperm from one bull may fertilise eggs in thousands of cows. Eggs from cows that show superior qualities may be harvested, fertilised in vitro and the embryos placed in surrogate cows. This protects the superior cow from the risks of pregnancy. Much animal breeding is concerned with productivity, for example:

- increasing milk production of cows
- increasing growth rates of pigs and beef cattle
- improving the quality of meat

Breeders who breed animals for show or for the pet trade are concerned with appearance and temperament.

Plant breeding

Plant breeders often wish to combine features from different varieties of the same species. Many commercial varieties of crop plant that give good yields at harvest do not have resistance to diseases or pests and cannot tolerate harsh environmental conditions, such as drought. These desirable features may be present in older cultivated varieties or in wild relatives of the crop plant. The breeder will cross different varieties by transferring pollen that contains the male gametes. Precautions are taken to make sure that the plants are not pollinated naturally. Often the flowers will have their anthers (that produce pollen) removed and they will be covered in bags to exclude pollen from other plants. Breeders collect the seed, sow it and check the next generation of plants for the desired features. The new hybrid plants are often crossed with commercial varieties to make sure that the new variety will have a good yield. This crossing back to commercial varieties continues for several generations. The breeders will only use the plants that combine the desired qualities, for example disease resistance and high yield. Breeding programmes continue for up to 10 years before new varieties are made commercially available.

Examiner tip

In selective breeding, humans are the agents of selection. In natural selection, aspects of the environment are the agents of selection (see Module 3).

Hybrid refers both to the results of a cross between varieties and crosses between species. Most hybrids between species are infertile, but some are fertile and can therefore reproduce. Hybrids between varieties of the same species are fertile.

Environmental factors

There are many components to high productivity. Genes control different aspects of growth and development that interact in the production of muscle (meat), milk and eggs. In plants, genes control different stages of growth and the final yields of roots, seeds, fruits or other harvested parts. But these aspects of productivity are also influenced by the environment. Factors such as those listed in Table 8 make a huge difference.

Knowledge check 15

The use of antibiotics as growth promoters in animal production is banned in the EU. Suggest why a ban was introduced.

Table 8 Ways in which farmers improve the environment for their crops and livestock to increase productivity

Crop plants	Livestock
Provide more light, e.g. use lamps in greenhouses	Provide better nutrition, e.g. formulated feeds
Provide more water by irrigation	Provide food supplements, e.g. vitamins, minerals, protein at appropriate times
Provide more carbon dioxide, e.g. burn propane in greenhouses	Provide protected environments, e.g. sheds, barns
Control pests and diseases with pesticides	Control pests and diseases with pesticides, antibiotics and vaccinations
Control competitors (weeds) by ploughing and using herbicides	Protect from predators
Provide mineral nutrients in the form of fertilisers	Use antibiotics in animal feed to promote growth (permitted in USA, banned by the EU from January 2006)
Plant hormones are sprayed onto some crops to improve their quality, e.g. seedless grapes	Use growth-promoting hormones in meat and milk production (permitted in USA, banned in the EU)

Fertilisers

Crop plants absorb ions, such as nitrate, phosphate, potassium, magnesium and sulfate from the soil. At harvest, many of these mineral nutrients are removed in the crop. Some crop residues will be left to decay so that some minerals return to the soil, but over time the mineral content of the soil decreases. This is especially rapid where the same crop is grown in the same place year after year. If the minerals are not replaced, yields will decrease. Adding organic matter, such as manure, that decays in

Examiner tip

Artificial fertilisers are also known as chemical fertilisers. The Haber process is used to fix nitrogen gas from the air to make fertilisers that provide nitrate ions.

the soil is the traditional method and is employed by organic farmers. Adding artificial fertilisers also allows farmers to maintain soil fertility; careful choice of fertiliser and time of application means that minerals can be added in the right quantities when the plants need to absorb them, without becoming an environmental problem.

Pesticides

Crop plants provide food for pests and diseases and they compete with weeds for light, water and mineral nutrients. Farmers have a large armoury of chemical pesticides to use. These include:

- fungicides to control fungal diseases
- molluscicides to control slugs and snails that eat crops, especially young seedlings
- insecticides to control insect pests that feed on roots, stems, leaves, fruits
- herbicides to control weeds that compete with crop plants for light energy and raw materials

Organic farmers do not use chemicals to control diseases, weeds and pests. By growing different crops in each field from year to year, pests and diseases tend to be less of a problem. These farmers also encourage natural predators of pests by growing wild flowers in field margins, retaining hedgerows and making temporary banks so that predatory beetles can range widely throughout the crop. All farmers are now encouraged to rely less on chemical methods to control pests and weeds because of adverse effects on wildlife and problems with pesticide resistance.

Links

Energy flows in ecosystems from the sun through plants to animals and decomposers. Energy is lost along food chains as organisms respire and this energy is transferred by heating the surrounding air or water. Energy is not recycled. Elements, such as nitrogen, phosphorus and sulfur are recycled. These elements are in organic compounds — amino acids, proteins, fats — that you read about earlier in this book. There are finite quantities of these elements available on the Earth and they must be recycled if life is to continue. You will learn more about energy flow and recycling at A2 in Unit F215.

Food and microorganisms

Key concepts you must understand

Microorganisms are used in the production of a variety of foods and drinks, such as yoghurt, cheese and beer. These microorganisms use biological processes that we understand and can modify. An understanding of the same biological principles helps us to control the microorganisms that cause **food spoilage**.

Key facts you must know

The advantages of using microorganisms in food production are as follows:

- Fast growth gives high yields.
- Growth is not dependent on seasons — production can occur throughout the year.

- Waste materials from other industries are used as substrates.
- Factories containing fermenters are not as extensive as farms and can be established where the necessary infrastructure and raw materials exist.
- It is much faster and easier to carry out selective breeding and genetic engineering on microorganisms than with domesticated plants and animals.
- There are fewer ethical issues than with keeping livestock, although some people object to the use of genetically modified organisms in their food.
- Quorn™, a meat-like food made from the fungus *Fusarium venenatum*, is very low in fat and is useful for people who want to reduce their intake of saturated fat from animal products.

The disadvantages are as follows:

- Bacteria and fungi can be infected by viruses — if this happens, then the production plant is shut down and sterilised.
- If other bacteria enter the fermenter, they may compete with the bacteria being cultured, so yields are lowered, the product may need more purification treatment and therefore costs increase.
- It is often difficult to market a novel food and sales may be low; there may be confusion between mycoprotein and genetically modified organisms. *F. venenatum* has never been genetically modified.
- Processing costs may be high and reduce the profit margin for foods made from microorganisms. For example, *F. venenatum* is high in nucleic acids (DNA and RNA), which have to be removed before the food is safe. Purines in the nucleic acids are metabolised in the body to uric acid, which can cause gout.

Food spoilage

Microorganisms (fungi and bacteria) are responsible for food going 'off'. At various stages in the human food chain, our foods are susceptible to being contaminated by microorganisms and vast quantities are lost every year to these decomposer organisms. These food spoilage organisms need the following in order to grow:

- a substrate — organic material (our food)
- water
- a suitable temperature
- oxygen (but not in all cases)
- a suitable pH

Examiner tip

When explaining methods of food preservation, you may need to refer to the effects of extremes of temperature and pH on enzyme activity.

The preservation methods listed in Table 9 remove one or several of these conditions for growth except, of course, the organic material.

Table 9 Methods of food preservation and the biological principles involved

Food preservation method	Example	Biological principle
Salting Syruping using sugar	Salted fish Tinned fruit and jams	Spoilage organisms cannot obtain water because the salt and sugar create a very low water potential in the foods
Pickling	Sauerkraut (pickled cabbage)	Enzymes in spoilage organisms are denatured by the low pH of the vinegar (ethanoic acid)
Heat treatment (pasteurisation)	Milk, wine	Food raised to 71.7°C for 15 seconds, then cooled; this kills potential pathogens (e.g. *Mycobacterium*) but not all bacteria

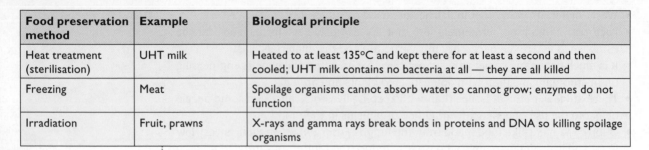

Food preservation method	Example	Biological principle
Heat treatment (sterilisation)	UHT milk	Heated to at least 135°C and kept there for at least a second and then cooled; UHT milk contains no bacteria at all — they are all killed
Freezing	Meat	Spoilage organisms cannot absorb water so cannot grow; enzymes do not function
Irradiation	Fruit, prawns	X-rays and gamma rays break bonds in proteins and DNA so killing spoilage organisms

Summary

- A balanced diet provides energy and nutrients sufficient to maintain metabolism and good health. An unbalanced diet provides too much or too little of one or more nutrients and leads to malnutrition. Obesity is an example of malnutrition caused by consuming an unbalanced diet often rich in saturated fat. This is also linked with coronary heart disease.
- Cholesterol is synthesised by the liver for use throughout the body. It is transported to and from tissues by lipoproteins. High-density lipoproteins remove it from tissues; low-density lipoproteins deposit it in tissues, including the walls of arteries such as the coronary arteries. Increases in blood cholesterol concentration increase the risks of cholesterol deposition.
- Crop plants provide energy for humans either directly or indirectly via livestock. Improvement in crop plants and livestock continues to be achieved by selective breeding for features such as higher growth rates, and disease and pest resistance.
- Fertilisers provide mineral ions (e.g. nitrate and phosphate ions) required by crop plants; pesticides are used to control plant pests, weeds and diseases; antibiotics are included in animal feed to increase food production (although their use is controversial).
- Microorganisms, such as fungi, are grown in fermenters to make human foods. Advantages are that production is not affected by climatic factors and the food produced can be made quickly if demand exists; disadvantages are that the fungal product is high in RNA that has to be removed during processing. This, and processing into products that people will buy, increases the cost.
- Food spoilage by fungi and bacteria is prevented by using salting and syruping (osmosis), pickling (pH), freezing and heat treatment (temperature) and irradiation (destruction of proteins and DNA).

Health and disease

Key concepts you must understand

Most of the topics on the next few pages concern disease rather than health. Both the terms 'health' and 'disease' are difficult to define, and you should be aware of this. However, here are some simple definitions:

- Health is physical, mental and social well-being. It is more than just being free from disease.
- Disease is a malfunction of the mind or body leading to a condition of poor health.

People who consider themselves 'healthy' because they are not suffering from the symptoms of a disease may have low physical fitness and may be developing a serious condition, such as heart disease or lung cancer.

Infectious diseases: malaria, tuberculosis (TB) and HIV/AIDS

Key concepts you must understand

Parasites live inside or on the surface of another organism known as the host. They obtain their energy from the host. Parasites that cause disease are called **pathogens**. The diseases that they cause are infectious diseases. Pathogens are transmitted from infected people to uninfected people. Since the late 1980s, there has been a pandemic of HIV/AIDS; tuberculosis (TB) is now on the increase worldwide, partly as a result of widespread HIV infection. Malaria has been a major killer disease probably for the whole of human history and is a huge medical and economic problem in many African and Asian countries.

Key facts you must know

Table 10 shows the organisms that cause these three diseases and how they are transmitted.

Table 10 Three infectious diseases, their causative organisms and methods of transmission

Disease	Causative organism	Type of organism	Methods of transmission
Malaria	*Plasmodium* species, e.g. *Plasmodium falciparum*	Protoctist (eukaryotic)	Female *Anopheles* mosquito (vector) takes a blood meal from an infected person; injects parasites in saliva when taking a blood meal from an uninfected person
Tuberculosis	*Mycobacterium tuberculosis* (also *M. bovis* from cattle)	Bacterium (prokaryotic)	Via droplets in the air — breathed out by infected person and breathed in by uninfected person; *M. bovis* in unpasteurised milk and undercooked meat, also direct contact with cattle
HIV/AIDS	Human immunodeficiency virus	RNA virus	From the bloodstream of an infected person to the bloodstream of an uninfected person during unprotected sexual intercourse; using shared needles; from mother to child — across the placenta, at birth and in breast milk; in donated blood or blood products

Global impact of malaria, TB and HIV/AIDS

The impact of these three diseases worldwide is huge in terms of human suffering and misery (Table 11).

Table 11 Global impact of malaria, TB and HIV/AIDS

Feature	Malaria	TB	HIV/AIDS
Worldwide occurrence	Tropics and sub-tropics	Worldwide	Worldwide, especially sub-Saharan Africa and Southeast Asia
Areas with highest prevalence (number of cases)	Sub-Saharan Africa	Russia, Asia, sub-Saharan Africa	Sub-Saharan Africa, South America, Southeast Asia
Prevalence worldwide in 2009	225 million	14 million	33.3 million
Annual worldwide mortality (2009)	781 000	1.3 million (TB alone without HIV)	1.8 million

Links

The differences between the structures of prokaryotic and eukaryotic cells are covered in Module 1 of Unit F211. *Mycobacterium* is a prokaryote. *Plasmodium* is a eukaryote with a much greater genetic complexity than prokaryotes. The surface antigens of *Plasmodium* change while in the human body and this makes it difficult to develop successful vaccines against malaria. HIV infects T-helper lymphocytes that control the immune response. HIV infection leads to a gradual loss of the ability to respond to pathogens. AIDS is a collection of different diseases that attack people who do not have a fully functional immune system. Two of these opportunistic diseases are a rare form of pneumonia and Kaposi's sarcoma, a rare cancer. TB is another.

The immune system

Key concepts you must understand

Our defence system consists of **primary defences** that are physical, chemical and cellular. These prevent entry of pathogens into the body. The second line of defence against pathogens involves chemical and cellular defences that are directed against the pathogens once inside the body. Phagocytes are part of our non-specific defence system that is not directed specifically at any one pathogen. They defend us by destroying invading organisms but they are not very effective on their own. Lymphocytes and antibodies are part of the specific defence system that recognises different pathogens and makes phagocytes more effective.

Key facts you must know

Primary defences

The skin forms an effective barrier to infection by pathogens. It consists of layers of dead cells filled with keratin, which is a tough fibrous protein. Some pathogens use vectors, such as mosquitoes, to gain entry through the skin. The gut, airways and reproductive system are lined by mucous membranes that consist of epithelial cells interspersed with mucus-secreting cells. Mucus is a slimy substance full of glycoproteins, which have long carbohydrate chains to make them sticky. Small particles in the air, such as bacteria, viruses, dust and pollen stick to mucus on the lining of the airways; cilia move mucus up the airways to the back of the throat. Cells in the lining of the stomach secrete hydrochloric acid that kills bacteria taken in with food. Cells along the length of the gut secrete mucus to protect the lining against attack by acid, enzymes and pathogens. These defences prevent entry of pathogens into the tissues and the blood. They also prevent pathogens growing inside the lungs, gut and reproductive system.

Cellular defences

Within the body there are two types of cell that are involved in defence:

- phagocytes
- lymphocytes

Both types of cell originate in bone marrow. These, and other blood cells, are shown in Figure 29. Figure 30 illustrates the origin and maturation of the cells involved in immunity.

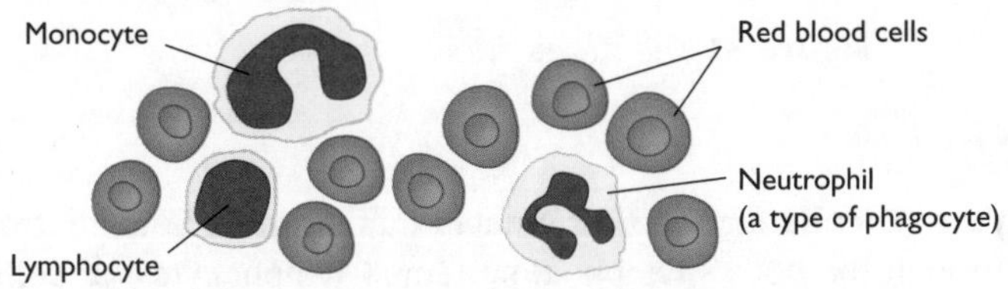

Figure 29 The different types of blood cell

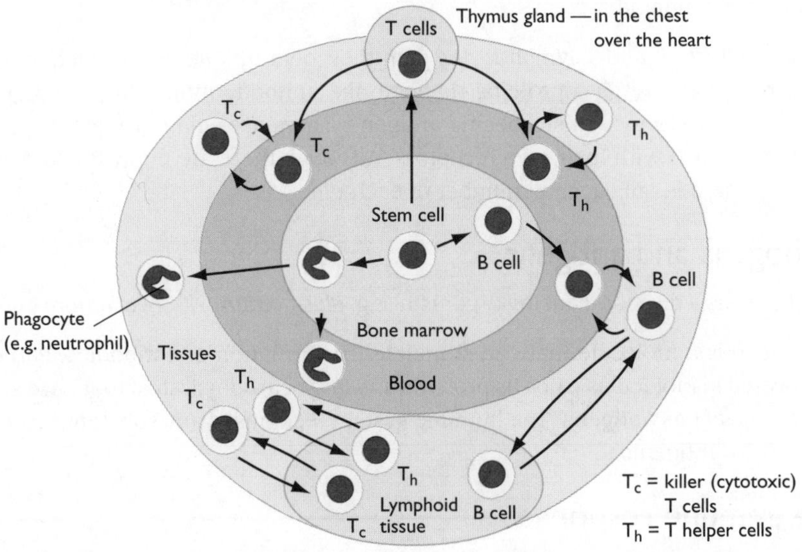

Figure 30 The origin and maturation of the major types of cell involved in immunity

Examiner tip

Figure 30 summarises the information about the origin and movement through the body of the different cells involved in both the non-specific and specific immune systems. There is a lot of information here. You could redraw the diagram on a large sheet of paper and annotate it fully.

Phagocytes

There are two types of phagocyte — neutrophils and monocytes/macrophages.

Neutrophils circulate in the blood and spread into tissues during an infection. They are the 'rapid reaction force' of the immune system, responding quickly by rushing to an infected area and attempting to destroy any pathogens in the tissues. They do not last long. After engulfing bacteria and destroying them, neutrophils die and sometimes accumulate to form pus.

Monocytes pass out of the bloodstream and enter tissues where they form **macrophages** (literally 'big eaters'). They are long-lived cells that have special roles to play in the immune response.

Phagocytosis is illustrated in Figure 31.

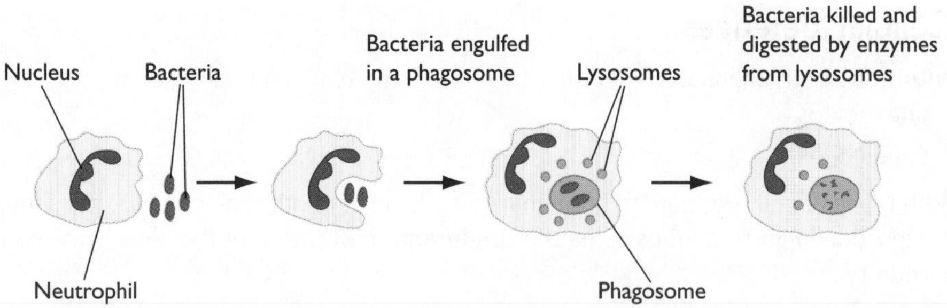

Figure 31 The stages involved in phagocytosis

Lymphocytes

B lymphocytes (**B cells** for short) originate and mature in bone marrow and then spread out through the body's lymphoid system. T lymphocytes (**T cells**) originate in bone marrow and migrate to the thymus where they mature. They then spread out through the lymphoid system.

As they mature, B and T lymphocytes gain their own unique cell surface receptors. These receptors are glycoproteins that are like antibody molecules. They give the cells the ability to recognise specific antigens. There are small groups of specific B and T cells, each with their own receptors. Although there are many B and T cells in the body, there is only a small number of each type.

Pathogens and antigens

A pathogen is a disease-causing organism (e.g. *Plasmodium*, *Mycobacterium* and HIV).

An antigen is a molecule that can stimulate the formation of antibodies. Pathogens are covered in molecules (such as proteins and large carbohydrates) that have specific shapes and act as antigens. The immune system recognises any substance foreign to the body as antigenic.

The immune response

Figure 32 shows the four stages in an immune response to a pathogen that has entered the body for the first time.

Stage 1 Antigen presentation

Macrophages in lymph nodes engulf pathogens by endocytosis and then 'cut them up'. These macrophages process antigens from the surface of the pathogen and put them into their own cell surface membranes.

Stage 2 Clonal selection

B cells and T cells with receptors complementary in shape to antigens lock onto the macrophage. These small groups of specific B and T cells are the clones that are selected by the macrophage.

Stage 3 Clonal expansion

As there are few B and T cells that are able to destroy the invading pathogen, the cells in these clones divide by mitosis to form much larger clones. T helper cells promote cell division by releasing hormone-like chemicals called cytokines to stimulate B cells to divide.

Stage 4 Antibody production

The stimulated B cells form plasma cells, which secrete the appropriate antibody.

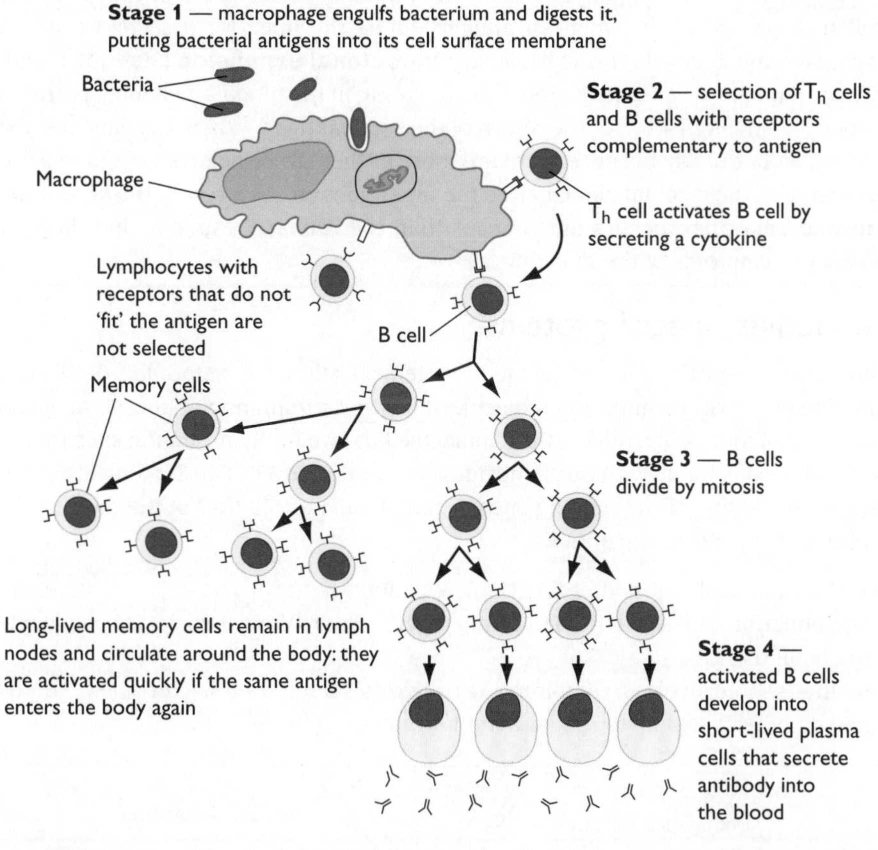

Figure 32 The stages of an immune response in which antibodies are produced

Viruses remain in the blood for a short time before they invade our cells. This means that antibodies against viruses do not work well because they are only effective when viruses are in the blood plasma. Antibodies are big molecules that cannot cross cell membranes to combine with viruses inside our cells. Some bacteria (e.g. the TB bacterium) invade cells too. These intracellular pathogens often produce proteins that are expressed in host cell surface membranes, so indicating that the cells are

Examiner tip

The release of cytokines is an example of cell signalling that you learned about in Unit F211. Cytokines have shapes that are complementary to those of receptors on the cell membranes of B cells.

Examiner tip

Antigen, antibody and antibiotic are easily confused. An **antigen** is a compound that stimulates antibody production; an **antibody** is a protein produced by B cells in response to a specific antigen; **antibiotics** are medicinal drugs used to treat bacterial infections.

infected. During an immune response, killer (cytotoxic) T cells may be selected and stimulated to divide by mitosis so that they attack host cells that express these antigens. Activated killer T cells attach to the surface of infected host cells and kill them by releasing toxic chemicals and enzymes.

Stages 1–4 take several days when an antigen enters the body for the first time — this is the **primary immune response**. This is why we are ill when we catch an infectious disease, such as measles. But after a while, antibodies and activated killer T cells are produced that help to remove the infectious agent and we recover. The whole process is much more efficient the next time because of memory cells.

Knowledge check 16

Explain the role of memory cells in long-term immunity.

Intracellular means inside cells; **extracellular** means outside cells. See the section on enzymes where these terms were also used.

Memory cells in long-term immunity

Plasma cells do not live long and soon the antibody molecules that they make are broken down. However, when an antigen enters the body for a second time, the response is much faster. This is because during **clonal expansion** (Stage 3), B and T cells form memory cells. These remain circulating in the blood and lymph, patrolling the body 'on the look out' for the return of the same antigen. When this happens, they respond more quickly because there are more of them to be selected in stage 2 than there were of the original clone before the first infection. As a result, the **secondary immune response** occurs much faster than the primary response and there are rarely any symptoms of the infection.

Knowledge check 17

Describe how the secondary immune response differs from the primary immune response to the same antigen.

Antibodies: special proteins

It helps here to recall your knowledge of protein structure from Module 1 of this Unit. The simplest form of antibody molecule (known as immunoglobulin G, or IgG) is composed of four polypeptides. Each molecule has two antigen-binding sites that are identical — each binds with the same antigen (see Figure 33). This binding is possible because the shape of the binding sites is complementary to that of the antigen. The antibody is specific to the antigen.

Two ways in which antibodies function are as follows:

- agglutination causes bacteria to clump together, so making it easier for phagocytes to engulf them
- neutralisation involves combining with toxins secreted by bacteria (e.g. tetanus and diphtheria toxins) to render them harmless

Examiner tip

Figure 33 is a simple diagram of an antibody molecule. You will get a much better idea of the fit between an antigen and the binding sites of an antibody if you find a 3D model, make your own from modelling clay or watch an animation.

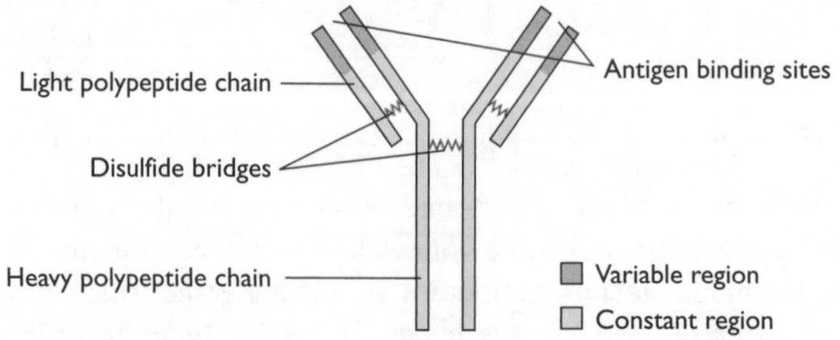

Figure 33 The structure of an antibody molecule (IgG)

We make many antibody molecules with different binding sites to 'fit' around the different antigens that invade us. This is possible because amino acids can be arranged in different sequences to give a range of three-dimensional shapes. Because these binding sites vary, they are also called **variable regions**. The **constant region** is the same for all IgG antibodies and fits into the receptors on phagocytes. This helps them to detect pathogens that have been 'labelled' by antibodies for destruction by phagocytosis.

Different types of immunity

So far we have considered what happens when an antigen enters the body. This is **active immunity** (see Figure 34). It may happen naturally when you are infected or it may happen artificially when you are given a preparation, or **vaccine**, containing an antigen. Active immunity always involves an immune response.

It is possible to receive antibodies from another person. This is **passive immunity** (see Figure 35) There is no contact with the antigen and no immune response occurs. Passive immunity is gained naturally when antibodies cross the placenta or are in breast milk. Injecting antibodies following snake bite is an example of gaining passive immunity artificially.

Knowledge check 18

State three ways in which active immunity differs from passive immunity.

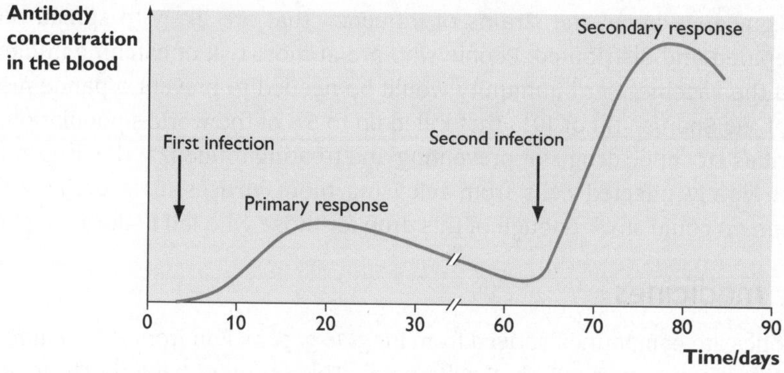

Figure 34 The change in antibody concentration during the primary and secondary response to the same antigen. This is what happens during active immunity.

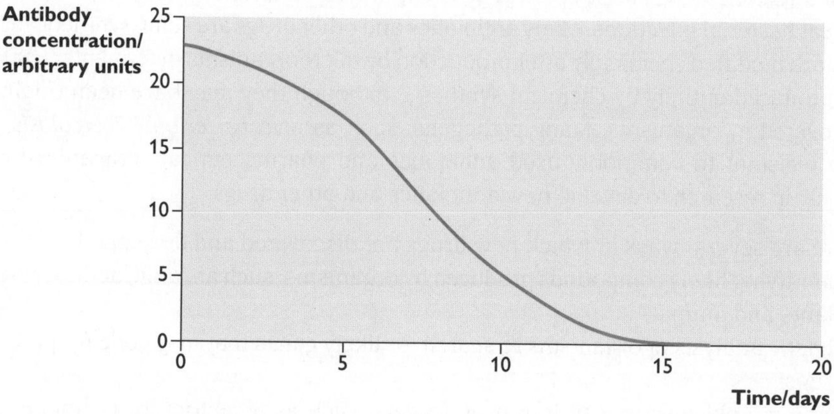

Figure 35 The change in antibody concentration in passive immunity. A person has been injected with antibodies. The concentration of antibodies decreases gradually because they are foreign to the body and are gradually removed. There are no activated lymphocytes (plasma cells) to secrete the antibody.

Vaccination controls disease

Vaccination is artificial active immunity. It can be used in two ways:

Examiner tip
Children are vaccinated against diseases, such as measles, to give herd immunity. Ring vaccination was used in the eradication of smallpox. Transmission of the disease was halted by vaccinating people in areas where cases had been identified.

- **herd immunity** — as many people as possible are vaccinated so that a pathogen cannot easily be transmitted from an infected person to an uninfected person because everyone, or nearly everyone, is immune. Vaccination programmes attempt to achieve nearly 100% coverage to achieve good herd immunity.
- **ring immunity** — people living or working near someone infected (or their contacts) are vaccinated to prevent them catching the disease and then spreading it.

People who are vaccinated cannot harbour the pathogen and cannot pass it on to others. This breaks the transmission cycle.

In 2008, the UK government announced that the greatest risk facing the population was an influenza pandemic. Influenza is a viral disease. The virus infects cells lining the trachea and bronchi. The cells become 'factories' for producing more viral particles which are released to infect more cells and to be transmitted when infected people cough and sneeze. We have a variety of non-specific responses to influenza, including inflammation of the airways.

Examiner tip
You may be asked to discuss the steps that governments should take when there is an epidemic. You could discuss who should have priority if the vaccine and the drug are rationed.

The virus may 'cross-breed' with viruses that cause similar diseases in animals or a strain that is pathogenic in animals may cross the species barrier and infect us. The World Health Organization (WHO) and national governments maintain a watch for new strains of the virus to which people have not been exposed. Each year, WHO issues guidance about the strains of influenza that are likely to spread. Vaccines are prepared and distributed. People who are at most risk of catching influenza are offered the vaccine. Herd immunity would be needed to prevent a pandemic on the scale of the Spanish flu of 1918 that killed up to 5% of the world's population. Health authorities stockpile drugs for preventing and treating influenza; the drug zanamivir inhibits virally infected cells from releasing more viruses. It is unlikely that the government could stock enough of this drug for those who fall ill during a pandemic.

Knowledge check 19
Explain why the same vaccine for influenza is not used year after year.

New medicines

Antibiotics are compounds derived from fungi (e.g. penicillin from *Penicillium*) or from the actinobacteria, particularly *Streptomyces*. This group of bacteria is the source of most antibiotics, such as streptomycin, erythromycin and tetracycline, which are used to treat bacterial infections. Many antibiotics and other drugs are semi-synthetic in that they are modified chemically after production by microorganisms in fermenters or they are produced entirely by chemical synthesis, although they may have been originally discovered in organisms. Many pathogens, such as *Mycobacterium tuberculosis*, are now resistant to commonly used antibiotics and pharmaceutical companies invest heavily in research to develop new antibiotics and other drugs.

Knowledge check 20
Distinguish between an antibiotic and an antibody.

There are several ways in which new drugs are discovered and developed:

- identifying likely compounds produced by organisms, such as fungi, actinobacteria, plants and animals
- genetic analysis of organisms to search for likely genes that may code for potential drugs
- finding molecules that fit into drug targets, such as receptors for hormones and receptors for neurotransmitters at synapses
- modifying existing drugs using computer modelling of the molecular structure of the drug and its target molecule.

Some examples of sources of new medicines are as follows:

- Marine actinobacteria have been discovered to be a source of rifamycin — an antibiotic effective against bacteria as it inhibits protein synthesis.
- *Calophyllum lanigerum*, a rare tree from the rainforest in Malaysia, is the source of calanolide A — a drug that stops HIV entering the nuclei of healthy T lymphocytes. This prevents the T cells producing new viruses and therefore decreases the spread of HIV throughout the body.

Plants used in traditional medicines are likely to make good potential medicines; many drugs in use today are derived from plants. It is likely that animals too may be sources of new drugs. This is one reason why it is important to conserve the world's biodiversity.

Examiner tip

These are examples of new medicines. You may know about others. Be prepared to write about examples that you know well.

Links

Stem cells in bone marrow develop into red and white blood cells. There is more about this in Module 1 of Unit F211. Phagocytosis is a form of endocytosis that you studied in the same module.

Antibodies like the IgG molecule shown in Figure 33 show all four levels of organisation of protein molecules. Remember that quaternary structure is having more than one polypeptide. The 3D shape of protein molecules is crucial here in giving the specific shape to the variable region, so that it fits around the antigen. The shapes of the antigen and antibody are complementary to each other in the same way as with an enzyme and its substrate. This makes an antibody *specific* to its antigen.

Smoking and disease

Key concepts you must understand

Before starting this section you should review what you learned about gas exchange in Unit F211. This section is about the effects of cigarette smoke on the gaseous exchange and cardiovascular systems. Smoking causes lung cancer and chronic obstructive pulmonary disease (chronic bronchitis and emphysema). Smoking is involved in the development of cardiovascular diseases, such as stroke and coronary heart disease. It is also implicated in many other diseases, such cancers of the mouth, oesophagus and bladder.

Examiner tip

Make sure you know the difference between the gaseous exchange system and the cardiovascular system. Confusing them will lose you marks when answering questions on the effects of smoking.

Key facts you must know

Cigarette smoke has over 4000 substances in it. The important constituents are:

- tar — a black, oily liquid which settles in the bronchi and bronchioles
- carcinogens — cancer-causing chemicals, e.g. benzopyrene
- carbon monoxide — a gas that combines with haemoglobin
- nicotine — the drug in tobacco that is absorbed into the blood

The effects of tar and carcinogens from tobacco smoke on the gaseous exchange system are shown in Figure 36. The effects of carbon monoxide and nicotine are shown in Figure 39.

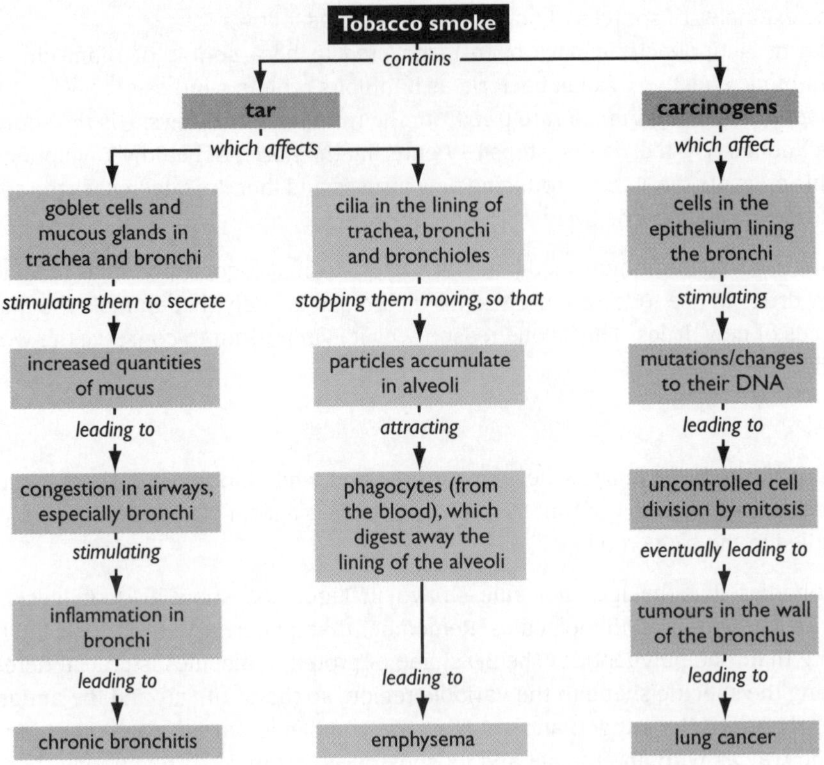

Figure 36 The effects of tar and carcinogens from tobacco smoke on the gaseous exchange system

Long-term smoking causes progressive changes in the linings of the airways, particularly in the bronchi (see Figure 37). Emphysema occurs when the walls of the alveoli are broken down by white blood cells that invade the air spaces to destroy bacteria and particles that have been carried by the air and not removed by the mucus and cilia in the bronchi and bronchioles. Figure 38 shows the effects of emphysema on lung structure.

Knowledge check 21

Explain how cigarette smoking may lead to lung cancer.

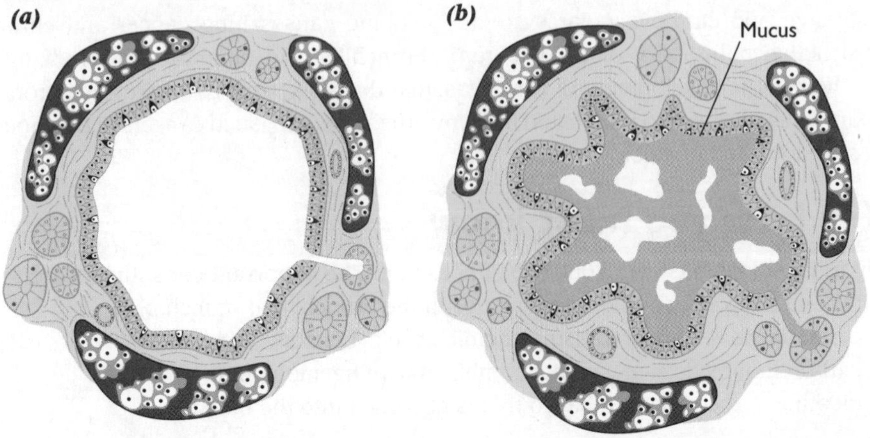

Figure 37 Cross-section of a bronchus of (a) a non-smoker and (b) a smoker. The smoker has bronchitis.

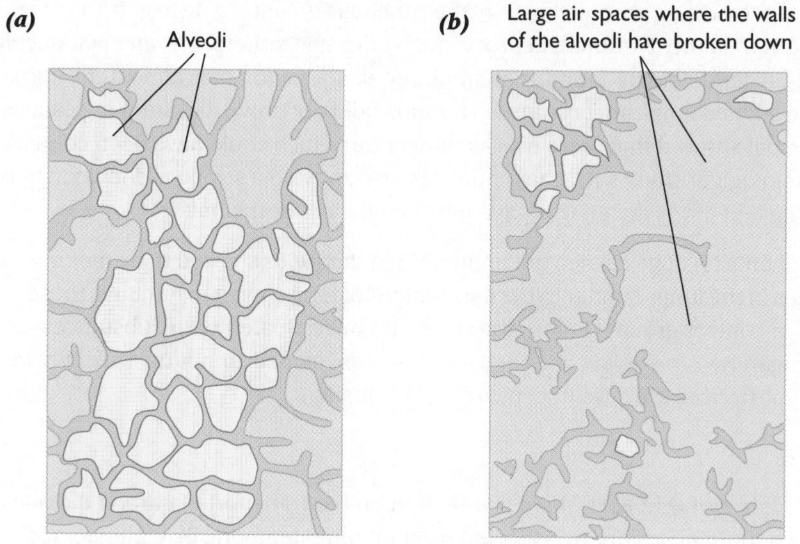

Figure 38 Cross-section of lung tissue of (a) a non-smoker and (b) a smoker. The smoker has emphysema.

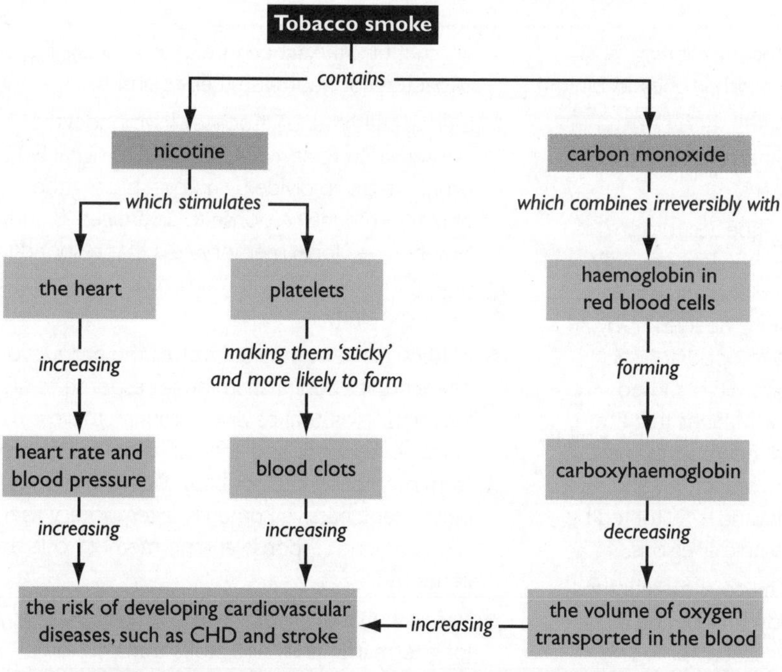

Figure 39 The effects of nicotine and carbon monoxide from tobacco smoke on the cardiovascular system

Evidence linking smoking with lung cancer

There are two lines of evidence:

- epidemiological — from studies of patterns of disease
- experimental — from controlled experiments carried out in the laboratory

Lung cancer was a rare disease in the nineteenth century. It began to increase in the UK in the early twentieth century and by the 1950s there was an epidemic. In the 1950s, epidemiologists found that smoking was a factor that almost all the people who developed lung cancer shared. This alone did not prove that smoking causes lung cancer, but showed that there was a connection, which could have been coincidental. Epidemiological studies in other countries also showed a strong association between smoking and lung cancer; this gave much evidence for the link.

Knowledge check 22

Explain the limits of epidemiological evidence.

Experiments on dogs carried out in the USA in the 1960s showed that smoking caused changes in the lungs similar to the early stages of lung cancer in humans; these did not occur in control groups. Laboratory rats and mice treated with substances isolated from cigarette smoke, such as benzopyrene, developed tumours. This showed that these substances are carcinogenic (cancer-causing).

Links

In Module 2 of Unit F211, there is a section on the transport of carbon dioxide and oxygen. Both gases are transported by combining temporarily with haemoglobin. Carbon monoxide combines permanently with haemoglobin, reducing the quantity of oxygen carried by 5–10%. Figure 39 shows the effects of carbon monoxide (and nicotine) on the cardiovascular system.

Summary

- Health is physical, mental and social wellbeing. Disease is a malfunction of the mind or body leading to a condition of poor health.
- Parasites live in or on host organisms. Those that cause disease are called pathogens.
- Malaria is caused by *Plasmodium* species that are transmitted by female *Anopheles* mosquitoes. HIV is transmitted by blood-to-blood contact, e.g. during unprotected sex, by sharing needles or by blood transfusion; HIV is linked to opportunistic infections that develop into AIDS. TB is caused by *Mycobacterium tuberculosis* or *M. bovis* that are transmitted in droplets and inhaled into the lungs, or through bovine products or contact. TB and AIDS are important globally; malaria is restricted by its method of transmission to tropical regions.
- Primary defences are skin and mucous membranes that prevent entry into the body. Phagocytes in blood and tissues ingest and digest bacteria. The immune system provides a highly specific defence against pathogens. During an immune response, specific B lymphocytes are activated to secrete antibodies.
- Antibodies are proteins with quaternary structure. The specific shape of the variable regions of each type of antibody is complementary to an antigen to which it binds. Antibodies either cause agglutination of bacteria or neutralise their toxins.
- During an immune response, T lymphocytes are activated to secrete cytokines to signal B lymphocytes to divide by mitosis. During the primary immune response to an antigen, B and T lymphocytes form memory cells that respond faster during the secondary immune response, giving long-term immunity.
- Natural active immunity involves the production of antibodies during an immune response to an infection. In natural passive immunity there is no immune response and antibodies are transferred from mother to fetus or baby. Active immunity is permanent; passive immunity is temporary as there is no immune response and no memory cells are produced.
- Vaccination is artificial active immunity that provides long-term immunity and stops transmission of pathogens in populations. Injection of antibodies provides immediate, but short-term artificial passive immunity.
- Governments coordinate the response to threats of new strains of influenza by ensuring the provision of suitable vaccines and drugs.

- Drug research involves screening microorganisms and plants for likely useful compounds. This is a reason for maintaining biodiversity.
- Smoking increases the risks of developing diseases of the gaseous exchange system: chronic bronchitis, emphysema and lung cancer.
- Nicotine and carbon monoxide in tobacco smoke are linked with diseases of the cardiovascular system: atherosclerosis, coronary heart disease and stroke.
- Epidemiological and experimental evidence shows that cigarette smoking is linked to diseases, such as lung cancer.

Module 3: Biodiversity and evolution

Biodiversity

Key concepts you must understand

At its simplest, biodiversity is a catalogue of all the species in an area, a country or even the whole world. But biodiversity also includes the diversity of habitats in an area and the genetic diversity within species. Much of this section is concerned with how biodiversity can be measured.

Key facts you must know

What is a species?

The definition of a species is often given as:

> A group of organisms able to interbreed and give rise to fertile offspring.

This definition describes a biospecies. When many species are described for the first time it is impossible to apply this definition because most are described using physical features, such as morphology (outward appearance) and anatomy. A different definition is used for a morphological species:

> A group of organisms that share many physical features that distinguish them from other species.

Local biodiversity

A species list gives an indication of the **species richness** of an area — how many species are present. The following is a species list of plants in an area of wasteland: daisy, dandelion, plantain, clover, buddleia, ragwort, spurge, stinging nettle, willowherb and groundsel.

Dichotomous keys are used to identify organisms. (Dichotomous means dividing into two pieces.)

Examiner tip

You should use some dichotomous keys to identify animals or plants. In the exam you may be given some drawings or photos of organisms to identify by using a key.

Counting the number of species is one way to assess biodiversity. Another is to look at the number of different habitats available in an area. A habitat is the place where an organism lives. Compare deciduous and coniferous woodland in the UK. An oak tree provides habitats for about 200 different species. In the spring, the ground beneath the tree is covered in ground flora — plants such as bluebell, *Hyacinthoides non-scripta*, and dog's mercury, *Mercurialis perennis*. The soil is rich in invertebrates including many earthworms. Coniferous woodland is dark all year round, has almost no ground flora and the soil has a low pH and few invertebrates. Coniferous woodland provides few habitats, so its biodiversity is low on two counts.

A species list is *qualitative*. It does not give us an idea of the number of each species and so cannot tell us which are common and which are rare. However, this qualitative information is useful, as areas with many different species tend to be more stable than those with only a few species. They are better, for example, at coping with environmental changes. So the second aspect of biodiversity is recording how many of each species are present — their abundance. The number of species and their abundance is another measure of biodiversity — **species evenness**.

Knowledge check 23

Distinguish between species richness and species evenness.

Recording the abundance of some plant species is relatively easy. For example, you can count the number of shrubs and trees present in a small area of woodland. Counting the number of birds can be difficult and it is impossible to count the individual grass plants in a lawn; so different methods are employed for different species. There is not enough space in this book to cover the methods employed, but you can find out about bird censuses at **http://www.bto.org/volunteer-surveys** and about plant surveys at **www.countrysideinfo.co.uk/howto.htm**.

Random sampling

Many of the plants that grow in waste ground are individual plants, so we can count individuals. It would take too long to count all the plants in the whole area, so we take representative samples. A quadrat is used to delimit an area of ground. Most quadrats are 0.5 m × 0.5 m or 0.25 m^2. We could do all our sampling at the easiest places to sample, but that would give a biased set of results. The easiest places to sample may have the fewest plant species, so random samples must be taken to avoid any bias on the part of the person doing the sampling. This can be done by placing tape measures at right angles to each other along two sides of the sample area. Random numbers are generated to give coordinates where the quadrats can be placed. The numbers of individual plants within the quadrat are counted and the information recorded in a table. When sampling plant species, it is often necessary to record percentage cover because it is impossible to see individual plants. In that case you estimate how much of the quadrat encloses each plant and express the answer as a percentage of the area of the quadrat.

Abundance data may be used to calculate the Simpson's index of diversity. There is a worked example of this in Question 6 on page 91. When the index is small (near 0) there is a very low diversity. When the number is high (near 1) there is a very high diversity

Global biodiversity

No one really has any idea of how many species there are on Earth. Estimates vary between 5 million and 30 million species. Some 1.75 million species have been properly described and have scientific names. There are various estimates and there are projects to catalogue information about living organisms in databases to aid research. You can find out more about these projects at the Tree of Life Project: **www.tolweb.org/tree/phylogeny.html**.

There are several reasons why no one knows. Even though amateur and professional biologists have been cataloguing species for hundreds of years, there are still places on Earth that have not been explored fully, such as the oceans and tropical forests. Also, scientists do not all agree on the species that have been described and often subdivide them or group them together.

Summary

- One definition of a species is a group of interbreeding organisms that produce fertile offspring. A habitat is a place where an organism lives. Biodiversity is the number of species in an area and the genetic variation within species. It also includes the variation in habitats and ecosystems in an area.
- Biodiversity in a habitat is assessed by random sampling, often using quadrats.
- Species richness is assessed by identifying all the species in a habitat; species evenness by assessing the abundance of each species in an area in terms of number per unit area or percentage cover.
- Simpson's index of diversity is a measure of biodiversity and uses both species richness and species evenness in the calculation. A high value (near 1) indicates an area with high biodiversity.
- Estimates of global biodiversity vary considerably because there are areas of the world that have not yet been sampled thoroughly and scientists do not always agree on whether organisms belong to the same species or to a different species.

Classification

Key concepts you must understand

Look on the back cover of this book and you will see an ISBN (International Standard Book Number) that identifies it, whichever country it is being sold in. This way of identifying books is similar to giving names to species. When cataloguing books in libraries, most follow the Dewey system for organising into categories and subcategories. Biologists have developed similar systems for classifying organisms.

Key facts you must know

In the eighteenth century, the Swedish biologist Carl Linnaeus (1707–78) devised the binomial system for naming species, which is still used today. Linnaeus gave every known species two names. Throughout this book, organisms are named using the binomial system. In any writing that you do, make sure you use scientific names, ensuring that the generic name begins with a capital letter and the specific name begins with a lower case letter, e.g. *Bellis perennis* (common daisy). In print these names are *italicised* but when handwritten they must be underlined. When a binomial has been used once, it may be shortened, e.g. *B. perennis,* so long as it does not cause any confusion. It is important to use the binomial system if you carry out your practical assessment in Unit F216 at A2 using ecological investigations. If you want to find out how to classify an organism go to **www.catalogueoflife.org**.

Examiner tip

The name given to each species is *both* names in the binomial. The second name should *not* be called the species name. Rather, it is known as the specific name that is unique to a species in the genus.

This binomial system usually tells us something about the species. The wood mouse is *Apodemus sylvaticus,* which translates as 'not house, wood', because it was always being confused (and still is) with the house mouse, *Mus musculus*.

Classification is the organisation of living things into groups that are arranged in a hierarchy. Taxonomy is the study of classification and the way in which features are used to group organisms. Linnaeus devised a hierarchical classification system in which large groups were continually subdivided down to the level of the species. His biggest group was the kingdom and there were two: the plant and animal kingdoms. Taxonomists have since developed his classification system much in the same way that librarians have had to incorporate new subjects into the Dewey system. Table 12 shows the classification of three species of mice.

Table 12 Hierarchical classification of three species of mice

Taxon	Wood mouse	House mouse	Macleay's marsupial mouse
Domain	Eukaryota	Eukaryota	Eukaryota
Kingdom	Animalia	Animalia	Animalia
Phylum	Chordata	Chordata	Chordata
Class	Mammalia	Mammalia	Mammalia
Order	Rodentia	Rodentia	Dasyuromorphia
Family	Muridae	Muridae	Dasyuridae
Genus	*Apodemus*	*Mus*	*Antechinus*
Species	*sylvaticus*	*musculus*	*stuartii*

Antechinus stuartii is a marsupial mouse that lives in Australia. It is carnivorous, unlike the other two species. Superficially it looks like a mouse, but is not closely related at all as you can see above.

As biologists began studying the microbial world, they discovered that organisms were built on two basic body plans: prokaryote and eukaryote. They also realised that Linnaeus's two kingdoms were not sufficient. There was so much diversity within these groups that in 1969 Robert Whittaker (1920–80) devised the five kingdom classification as shown in Table 13. (Note that viruses do not fit into this classification — they have their own system.)

Examiner tip

In Unit F211, you studied the difference between prokaryotic cells and eukaryotic cells. The prokaryotic cells you studied were from the bacteria domain. Archaeans have characteristics in common with both bacteria and eukaryotes, which suggests that they are similar to the very first organisms on Earth.

During the latter part of the twentieth century, scientists gained information on further features, such as molecular biology, biochemistry and cell structure. In the 1970s, bacteria were discovered living in extreme environments such as hot springs. These extremophiles, as they are called, share features with prokaryotes and eukaryotes. In 1990, Carl Woese introduced the **domain** as a new taxon above the level of the kingdom, giving greater weight to molecular biology (particularly the structure of ribosomal RNA) than to other features. The extremophiles were classified in a separate domain, the Archaea, which is at the same taxonomic level as the bacteria and the eukaryotes.

Classification systems reflect relationships between organisms. The species put into the same genus are related as they have similar features. In fact it can be difficult even for experts to identify individuals from species that are closely related and this is why identification keys are so important.

Table 13 Some of the features used to categorise organisms into the five kingdoms

Features	Kingdom				
	Prokaryotae (Monera)	**Protoctista**	**Fungi**	**Plantae**	**Animalia**
Type of body	Mostly unicellular	Unicellular and multicellular	Mycelium composed of hyphae; yeasts are unicellular	Multicellular, not compact	Multicellular; most have a compact body
Nuclei	✗	✓	✓	✓	✓
Cell walls	✓ (made of peptidoglycan)	Present in some species	✓ (made of chitin)	✓ (made of cellulose)	✗
Organelles and fibres (e.g. microtubules)	✗	✓	✓	✓	✓
Type of nutrition	Autotrophic and hetero-trophic	Autotrophic and heterotrophic	Heterotrophic	Autotrophic	Heterotrophic
Motility (ability to move themselves)	Some bacteria have flagella	Some protoctists have undulipodia or cilia	✗	✗	✓ (muscular tissue)
Nervous coordination	✗	✗	✗	✗	✓
Examples	Bacteria and cyanobacteria (blue greens)	*Amoeba*, algae, slime moulds	Mould fungi (e.g. *Aspergillus*), yeast	Liverworts, mosses, ferns, conifers, flowering plants	Jellyfish, coral, worms, insects, vertebrates

In the past, the only features that biologists could study were those they could see: the external appearance (known as morphology) and the internal structure (anatomy). In the nineteenth century, there was much discussion about the immutability of species — whether or not they could change over time. Classification systems then were based on physical features, often of dead specimens collected on expeditions by naturalists and explorers. Now other evidence is used, such as similarities and differences between the primary structures of proteins and the sequences of bases in genes.

Classification systems reveal the **phylogeny** of taxa because they group together organisms with many shared features. Phylogeny is the evolutionary history of organisms. Not all classification systems reflect phylogeny; some are purely utilitarian — people who write keys for amateur naturalists often first classify flowering plants according to the colour of the flowers and use this feature to make the key. Flower colour is not a feature that reveals phylogenetic links between groups of flowering plants.

Knowledge check 24

Define the terms taxon, hierarchy, binomial system and phylogeny.

Summary

- Classification is the organisation of organisms into a hierarchical system of groups or taxa; domain is the largest taxon, species the smallest. Phylogeny is the evolutionary history of a group, e.g. a species. Closely related species have many features in common, so classification systems often reflect their phylogeny.
- Organisms are classified into five kingdoms: Prokaryotae, Protoctista, Fungi, Plantae and Animalia. Each kingdom has a set of features of structure and function, such as methods of nutrition.
- Each species is given a binomial name: the first name is the genus (or generic) name and the second is the specific name. For example the binomial name for the African elephant is *Loxodonta africana.*
- Dichotomous keys are used to identify organisms.
- Classification systems were devised originally using observable features such as morphology (external appearance) and anatomy. Other evidence is now used such as similarities in the primary structure of proteins in different organisms and in the sequences of bases of genes.
- The three domain system identifies Bacteria, Archaea and Eukaryota as the largest groupings in hierarchical classification. It uses what are considered to be fundamental features such as aspects of molecular biology, e.g. aspects of RNA.

Evolution

Key concepts you must understand

When people talk about evolution they are usually referring to two distinct ideas:

- the general theory of evolution that states that organisms change over time
- the special theory that evolution occurs by the process of **natural selection**

In 1859, Charles Darwin published *On the Origin of Species*, the book that presents the special theory of natural selection with much supporting evidence. Although our ideas about natural selection have changed over the past 150 years, it remains the best explanation of the numerous observations made by scientists about species and how they change.

Key facts you must know

Variation is the sum of the differences between species and within species. **Interspecific** variation is the variation *between* species. This is used to identify species and to classify them as discussed in the previous section. **Intraspecific** variation is variation *within* species. This variation is the raw material for natural selection and is the variation discussed in this section.

If you look at different features of plants, animals and microorganisms, you can distinguish between two forms of intraspecific variation:

- **discontinuous variation** — distinct forms without any intermediates, e.g. human blood groups; red, pink and white flowers in the snapdragon, *Antirrhinum majus*; drug-resistant and drug-susceptible forms of *Mycobacterium tuberculosis*
- **continuous variation** — a range between two extremes, with no easily identifiable intermediate groups, e.g. mass and linear measurements of organisms (height of plants, width of leaves, tail length of mice, etc.)

It is sometimes quite difficult to decide whether a feature shows discontinuous or continuous variation. Remember that examples of discontinuous variation are *qualitative* and cannot be given a measurement, whereas examples of continuous variation can be measured and are *quantitative*.

When displaying data about continuous variation, it is necessary to divide the range into arbitrary groups and show the data as a histogram. For example, if you measure the tail length of a group of mice of different ages you can divide the results into different groups: 20 to 29 mm; 30 to 39 mm etc. and then plot them as a histogram. But you have to decide on the number and sizes of groups.

Data for discontinuous variation are already grouped into categories (A, B, AB and O blood groups, for example) and are shown as a bar chart, with each category represented by a bar separated from others by space on the graph paper.

Features that show discontinuous variation are controlled solely by genes; the environment has no effect. Features that show continuous variation are influenced both by genes and the environment. Consider the factors that determine the body mass of mice: availability of food, environmental temperature and quantity of stored fat. There are some genes that influence body mass; an allele of one of these genes gives rise to obese mice.

The technique of electrophoresis, which is similar to chromatography, reveals even more examples of variation between individuals. Figure 40 shows the results of an investigation into variation in liver enzymes in the house mouse, *Mus musculus*. The mixture of enzymes from each mouse was placed in a well cut into a slab of gel. In electrophoresis, an electric field is applied across the gel so that proteins move towards the anode because they are negatively charged. Each type of enzyme moves according to its mass. Small molecules move further than larger ones to form bands in the gel. The results show that there were seven of these enzymes, three that were present in all eight mice and four that were present only in some mice.

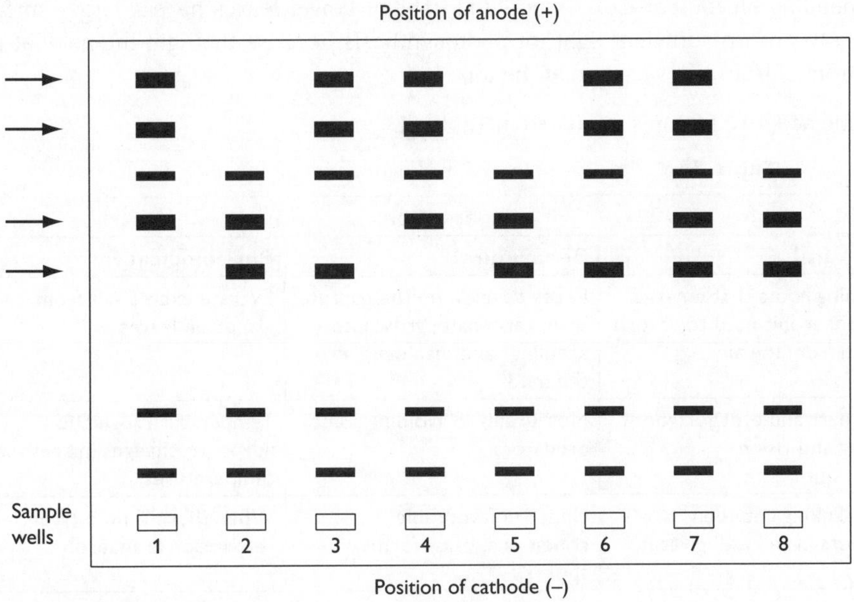

Figure 40 Separation of liver enzymes from *Mus musculus* mice. The arrows indicate the four enzymes that are present in some of these mice, but not all.

Examiner tip

There is advice about drawing histograms and bar charts (and line graphs) in the unit guide for Units F213/F216. You should follow the advice on drawing graphs and, when preparing for the quantitative and evaluative tasks, make sure you know how to interpret and describe them.

Knowledge check 25

Electrophoresis shows variation at the level of proteins. How many enzymes were present in all eight mice in the survey? How many mice had the enzyme with the smallest molecular size?

What are the causes of intraspecific variation in mice?

This tells us that there is variation in the enzymes in the different mice, which reflects differences in the genetics of these individuals. Each enzyme is coded for by a different gene. If the enzyme is missing, it means that the mouse in question has two alleles neither of which code for the enzyme. This shows that among the eight mice in the study there is genetic variation that gives rise to variation at the biochemical level. This may have an effect on how the mice survive in their environment and is an example of variation that exists within species — the variation that is the raw material for selection.

Adaptation

For an organism to exist successfully in an environment, it must possess features that help it to survive. Adaptation is the way in which organisms are suited to their environment. This includes their external appearance (morphology), internal structure (anatomy), the function of body systems (physiology), chemistry of cells (biochemistry) and behaviour, reproduction and life cycle. Measuring variation within species is one way in which adaptation can be assessed. Why do adult mice have tail lengths that are all nearly the same rather than a wide range from tiny tails to extremely long tails? Why do some woodland snails have brown shells, while others have pink ones? Why are leaves on the lower branches of trees larger than those at the top? These features are adaptive and studying them can tell us about the ways in which these organisms fit into their environment. You have to be able to outline the structural, behavioural and physiological features of organisms from the five different kingdoms. It is likely in an examination that you will read some information about the features of an organism or a group of organisms and be expected to explain how they are adaptive. The answers to the questions posed above are: mice use their tails for balance and very short (no use as a counterbalance) and very long (unwieldy) tails would not be suitable. Shell colour of woodland snails is related to camouflage, depending on the particular woodland habitat. Lower leaves have a larger surface area to absorb sufficient light for photosynthesis because the light intensity at the bottom of trees is lower than at the top.

Knowledge check 26

Explain what is meant by an *adaptive feature.*

Some adaptive features are listed in Table 14.

Table 14 Adaptations of species of plant, animal and microorganism

	Adaptation		
Species	**Structural**	**Behavioural**	**Physiological**
Black mangrove, *Avicennia germinans*, grows along muddy shores in the tropics	Breathing roots that emerge from anaerobic mud to absorb oxygen from the air	Seeds develop on the parent tree, germinate, grow into seedlings and *then* drop into the mud	Excrete excess salt from glands on leaves
Wood mouse, *Apodemus sylvaticus*	Large ears and eyes for good hearing and vision	Nocturnal, so avoiding some predators	Temperature regulation adapts to changes in seasonal temperatures
Yeast, *Saccharomyces cerevisiae*	Cross-linking between polymers in cell wall gives it rigidity	Under unfavourable conditions, yeast forms spores	When there is no oxygen, respiration is anaerobic

Darwin's observations

In developing his theory of natural selection, Darwin made four observations:

(1) All organisms reproduce to give far more offspring than are ever going to survive.

(2) Populations of organisms fluctuate, but they do not tend to increase and decrease significantly over time — they remain fairly constant.

(3) There is variation among the offspring — they do not look exactly like their parents or exactly like each other.

(4) Offspring resemble their parents. Features are transmitted from one generation to the next.

There are finite quantities of resources for organisms. Individuals of the same species need the same resources and have similar adaptations for gaining those resources. If there are more organisms than the environment can support, many will die, so that populations remain fairly constant from generation to generation. Some of the environmental factors that control the sizes of populations of heterotrophic organisms are food, water, disease and predation. Populations of autotrophs are controlled by disease and grazing, but also by access to light, carbon dioxide and water.

Struggle for survival

Individuals that are adapted to gain resources and avoid catching lethal diseases and being eaten are likely to be those that survive and reproduce to pass on their genes to future generations. These organisms are better adapted than others to the conditions prevailing at the time. They are selected by the environment as they have a selective advantage.

Every generation creates variation when it breeds to produce offspring. There are a number of ways in which this variation is generated, but **mutation** is the only way in which totally new genetic material is formed. You will learn about this and other causes of variation at A2 in Unit F215.

When the environment is stable, natural selection acts to maintain the features of a species, but if the environment changes then selection pressures in the environment change. This means that organisms showing some features that were previously less advantageous are now the ones that compete well, survive and breed. The generation of variation is necessary if this is going to happen and species are to adapt to changing conditions. This shows how variation, adaptation and selection are important components of evolution.

Here are some examples of selection acting on mice. Brown mice are visible to predators on a sandy beach where yellow fur is the best colour to have. Small, slender mice tend not to survive in cold climates because they have a large surface area-to-volume ratio and lose heat too quickly. Mice in colder regions tend to be larger than those in warmer regions. Artificial selection in the house mouse, *M. musculus*, has given rise to a large number of strains that people keep as pets and are used in laboratories. Artificial selection has revealed much more variation than is obvious in wild populations that are exposed to environmental selection pressures.

Examiner tip
Darwin studied variation among wild and domesticated animals, such as pigeons, but he did not know how variation was brought about or inherited. When you have studied genetics in Unit F215 you will have the bigger picture about how selection influences the genes and alleles in populations of organisms.

Speciation is the formation of new species. This can happen when populations of the same species become separated by geographical barriers such as bodies of water or mountain ranges. Environmental conditions in the different areas are likely to be different, so different selection pressures exist. Over a period of time, the populations become adapted to different conditions and eventually the differences between them mean they cannot interbreed to produce fertile offspring; they are no longer the same species.

Evidence for evolution

Key concepts you must understand

Biologists look at remains of organisms from the past and research the environments in which they lived. This line of evidence shows that life on Earth is ancient, and by studying fossils we can follow the history of different groups of organisms. Study of organisms alive today reveals their ancestry or phylogeny. There are also a variety of sophisticated analytical methods that reveal evolutionary relationships, and evidence from biochemistry is helping to build a more detailed history of life on Earth. The use of antibiotics and insecticides has exposed pathogenic bacteria and insect pests to selection pressures, with important consequences for us.

Key facts you must know

Evidence from fossils

A fossil is a mineralised or otherwise preserved remains or trace (such as a footprint) of animals, plants, and other organisms. Fossils are found in sedimentary rocks and chemical traces of fossils are detected in metamorphic rocks. The oldest fossils are those of prokaryotes found in rocks that are 3.5 billion years old. Chemical traces of prokaryotes have been found in rocks even older than this, indicating that life is as old as 3.9 billion years.

In the Grand Canyon in Arizona, the Colorado River has cut a deep gorge through layers of rock. At the base there are fossils of prokaryotes that are 1250 million years old. Near the top there are fossils of more recent origin, including coral and molluscs that are 250 million years old. In the middle there are fossils of reptiles, amphibians and terrestrial plants. Fossils tell us that environments and organisms have changed over millions of years.

Biologists in the nineteenth and early twentieth century compared the morphology and anatomy of species to show evolutionary relationships. The pattern of bones in the front limbs in tetrapods (amphibians, reptiles, birds and mammals) is basically the same even though there are differences between them. This indicates that these animals had a common origin. Over the past 60 years or so a wide range of techniques has become available to take this study of similarities and differences among organisms much further.

Evidence from biochemistry

Many biological molecules are the same in all organisms — for example, DNA, RNA, ATP, proteins, phospholipids, polysaccharides and the coenzymes. This argues for a common ancestry for all life on Earth. Analysis of the amino acid sequences of proteins reveals that proteins from closely related organisms are very similar. The active site of an enzyme like catalase tends to be identical whatever organism it comes from as no other arrangement of amino acids gives the right three-dimensional shape to fit the specific substrate. But there are unlikely to be such constraints on other parts of the molecule; looking at enzymes from many organisms reveals differences, which become greater the less closely related they are.

The primary structure of proteins is determined by the sequences of bases in DNA. Nucleotide sequences in genes from closely related organisms are very similar.

Natural selection in action

Antibiotics became widespread in the late 1940s. They proved hugely successful in treating bacterial disease such as TB, but very soon antibiotics such as streptomycin became less effective as *Mycobacterium* developed antibiotic resistance. This happened because some bacteria possessed genes that coded for ways to prevent the effect of the antibiotic. Penicillin is effective because it prevents the growth of cell walls of some bacteria. Resistant bacteria have enzymes that can break down penicillin. When antibiotics are used, any resistant bacteria are clearly at an advantage as they are adapted to the new conditions. The susceptible forms die and the resistant bacteria survive and reproduce to pass on their genes to future generations. Selection has also happened to insect pests that have been sprayed with insecticides. Insects susceptible to insecticides have died, while resistant forms have survived and increased in number. In these examples, antibiotics and insecticides are **selective agents**.

Summary

- Variation is the difference between organisms. Interspecific variation is the sum of all differences between species; intraspecific variation is the sum of all variation within a species.
- Variation in a particular feature may be continuous or discontinuous. Continuous variation is variation in a quantitative feature, such as height, that exists between two extremes (e.g. tall and short); discontinuous variation is variation in a qualitative feature that has no numerical value, e.g. blood group.
- Features that show continuous variation is influenced by both genes and the environment. Features that show discontinuous variation is influenced only by genes.
- Organisms have behavioural, physiological and anatomical features that adapt them to their environment.
- Darwin made four observations from which he proposed that species evolve by natural selection.
- The formation of new species is known as speciation. This can occur when populations of a species are separated geographically and exposed to different selection pressures. Over time, the two populations cannot interbreed so they are different species.
- Fossil evidence shows that evolution has occurred over time. Evidence from similarities in DNA and molecules such as ATP show that organisms on Earth have a common origin.
- Variation is the raw material of evolution. In a population that reproduces sexually, each generation has individuals that show variation in many features. Selection acts on individuals; those that survive to reproduce and pass on their alleles are those that are better adapted to survive.
- Humans act indirectly as selective agents by using antibiotics and pesticides. This has led to the selection of bacteria with antibiotic resistance and insects with pesticide resistance. The consequence is that we have to develop new chemicals to control bacterial pathogens, and the insect pests that destroy crops and lead to food shortages.

Maintaining biodiversity

Key concepts you must understand

As we have seen, biodiversity exists on different levels. You need to understand first what the threats to biodiversity are and why we should act to maintain diversity — what are the reasons for doing so. Action is taken on the local, national and global scale.

Key facts you must know

Table 15 shows some of the many reasons why we should maintain biodiversity and populations of species.

Table 15 Reasons for maintaining biodiversity

Reasons for maintaining biodiversity	Examples
Economic	Natural ecosystems provide food and materials for human populations, e.g. fish and timber; they are also important for providing clean water, and in climate regulation, soil formation and treating waste Old cultivated varieties and wild varieties of crop plants may provide sources of genes and alleles for improving our crop plants in the future; old breeds of domesticated animals and their wild relatives may also be similar sources
Ecological	The loss of species leads to an imbalance in natural communities — for example, loss of top predators, such as lions, tigers and leopards, often leads to increase in herbivores, overgrazing, land degradation, erosion and loss of biodiversity
Aesthetic	Areas of natural wilderness and managed countryside are appreciated by many people as beautiful places; they should be conserved for future generations
Medical	Sources of new medicines
Ethical	Humans have a duty to conserve natural ecosystems and their biodiversity for future generations

Ways of maintaining biodiversity

Conservation is defined as keeping and protecting a living and changing environment with its biodiversity. The best way to conserve species is to conserve them in their habitats. This is conservation *in situ*.

Sometimes it is impossible to conserve a species in its natural habitat as that habitat is shrinking or there are so few specimens left in the wild that they must be removed to botanic gardens and zoos to ensure the species does not become extinct. This is conservation *ex situ*. Many botanic gardens have seed banks where seed is stored. Seeds are collected from the wild, sorted, dried and stored in very cold conditions. They are checked at intervals to see if they are still viable. This ensures a supply of plants for the future and also is a store of genetic biodiversity — an important store of genes and alleles for future breeding programmes or to use for genetically modifying plants of economic importance. It is also a store of plant material that may be useful in providing medicines for the future.

Examiner tip
You can find out about the work of the botanic gardens at Kew and Edinburgh at **www.kew.org/conservation** and **www.rbge.org.uk/science/conservation**.

Zoos maintain populations of endangered species. Jersey Zoo is involved with captive breeding and reintroduction projects involving tamarins from Brazil. Howletts and

Port Lympne in Kent breed lowland gorillas, *Gorilla gorilla*, and are introducing them to reserves in West Africa. Przewalski's horse, *Equus ferus przewalskii*, has been bred very successfully at Whipsnade Zoo and Marwell Zoo and animals transferred to Mongolia where this wild horse became extinct 30 years ago. Zoos cooperate so that breeding programmes generate genetic diversity to ensure that species do not become inbred — a risk when maintaining small populations.

Examiner tip

Each of the zoos mentioned has a website where you can read more about its work in conservation. You can expect questions on species unfamiliar to you; do not panic, the examiner will be asking about the general principles of conservation as outlined here.

International conservation

The trade in animals for the pet trade and in animal materials, such as ivory, is huge. Much of this is illegal. The **Convention on International Trade in Endangered Species of Wild Fauna and Flora** (**CITES**) is an international treaty that protects animals and plants from various forms of exploitation. Over 30000 animal and plant species are protected by being placed on one of three Appendices, of which Appendix 1 has the species most at risk of extinction. Some trade is permitted, but only in exceptional circumstances. Appendices 2 and 3 list those species that are less threatened with extinction, but may be so in the future if trade persists.

The **Convention on Biological Diversity** (**CBD**) was signed at the 1992 UN Conference on Environment and Development (UNCED) in Rio de Janeiro in Brazil (the 'Earth Summit') and ratified in 1993. Countries that are signatories have to establish plans to protect biodiversity, which include writing and implementing Biodiversity Action Plans (BAPs).

Knowledge check 27

What aspects of biodiversity should be considered in any biodiversity action plan?

Since 1998, Newbury in Berkshire has had a bypass. During the lengthy planning stages it was discovered that it would go through an area occupied by the rare Desmoulin's whorl snail, *Vertigo moulinsiana*. Approval for the road (in 1988) was declared illegal as no **Environmental Impact Assessment** (EIA) had been carried out. EIAs were introduced in the European Union in 1985. An EIA must include a description of the biology of the area to be affected by any development and must assess the significant impacts that developments may have on the local environment, including its biodiversity. **Agenda 21** is the global action plan for sustainable development that promotes the use of EIAs, which are now applied to development projects worldwide.

Summary

- Animal and plant species should be conserved for economic, ecological, ethical and aesthetic reasons.
- Global climate change has consequences for biodiversity because many plants and animals are adapted to specific conditions that are either changing now or may change in the future. There may be consequences for agriculture if crops can no longer survive where they are currently grown. Pathogens, such as the malaria parasite, may also spread into areas where it does not exist currently.
- Animal and plant species are conserved *in situ* in their natural habitats and *ex situ* in zoos and botanical gardens. Conservation is best *in situ* where the complex requirements of each species are provided in its natural habitat. If the habitat is destroyed, or is too small to support viable populations, then removal and captive breeding may be necessary.
- Seed banks maintain collections of seeds of many species, including those that are rare. These may be used in the future as sources of variation for breeding and for restoration of habitats.
- International cooperation is a vital part of conservation. CITES and the Rio Convention on Biodiversity are two such examples.
- Local authorities must consider environmental impact assessments when coming to decisions about planning applications for new housing, industry, roads, etc

Questions & Answers

The unit test

The examination paper will be printed in a booklet, in which you will write all your answers. The paper will have seven or eight questions, each divided into parts. These parts comprise several short-answer questions (no more than 4 or 5 marks each) and two questions requiring extended answers, for around 7 or 8 marks each. The unit test has a total of 100 marks and lasts 1 hour 45 minutes.

Command terms

You need to know how to respond to the various command terms used in the unit test. These are outlined below.

'Describe' and 'explain'

These do not mean the same thing. 'Describe' means give a straightforward account. You may be asked to describe something on the paper, such as a graph. You may have to describe a structure or 'tell a story', for example by writing out the sequence of events in DNA replication. If you are describing what is shown in a graph or a table, you can often gain marks by quoting the data. 'Explain' means give some *reasons* why something happens. 'Explain how...' means that you should show the way something functions. 'Explain why...' is asking you to give reasons for something, such as an event or outcome.

'Name', 'identify' and 'state'

These all require a very concise answer, maybe just one word, a phrase or a sentence.

'Calculate' and 'determine'

Expect to be tested on your numeracy skills. For example, the examiner may ask you to calculate a rate of reaction, a percentage, a percentage change or the magnification of a drawing or photograph. 'Determine' means more than just calculate. You may be asked to explain how measurements should be taken and how a final answer is calculated. You may be asked how to determine Simpson's index of diversity or calculate the index from some data provided by the examiner.

'Outline'

This means give several different points about the topic without concentrating on one or giving lots of detail.

'Draw', 'sketch' and 'complete'

'Draw' and 'sketch' mean draw something on the examination paper, such as a sketch graph, a drawing or a diagram. 'Complete' means that there is something that you need to finish, such as a table, diagram or graph. You will not be expected to draw a graph on the examination paper, but you may have to put a line on a pair of axes to show a relationship.

'Differences'

If you are asked to give some 'differences', then it is likely that you will be asked to say how 'A differs from B'. The examiners will assume that anything you write will be something about A that is not the same as for B. Sometimes the examiner will give you a table to complete to show differences and then you will have to write something about both A and B.

Prepare yourself

Make sure that you have two or more blue or black pens, a couple of sharp pencils (preferably HB), a ruler, an eraser, a pencil sharpener, a watch and a calculator.

When told to start the paper, look through all the questions. Find the end of the last question. Find and read the questions that require extended answers. Some points may come to mind immediately — write them down before you forget.

There is no need to start by answering question 1, but the examiner will have set something quite straightforward to help calm your nerves. Look carefully at the number of marks available for each question. Do not write a lengthy answer if there are only 1 or 2 marks available. If you want to change an answer, then cross it out and rewrite the answer clearly. Always write within the box printed on each page. If you use the lines printed at the end of the exam paper for a continuation answer, indicate clearly that you have done this.

When you reach the questions that require extended answers:

- plan out what you intend to write and make sure it is in a logical sequence
- look at the examiner's instruction, which will be printed in italics — this tells you what you should do to gain the mark for quality of written communication
- do not write out the question
- keep to the point — you do not need an introduction or a summary
- use diagrams or sketch graphs if they help your answer — remember to label and annotate them
- pay careful attention to spelling, punctuation and grammar

Time yourself. Work out where you expect to be after 60 minutes. Leave yourself at least five minutes to check your paper to make sure you have attempted all the questions and have left nothing out. The best way to do this is to check the mark allocation — have you offered something for each mark?

You can expect questions to cover more than one module of the unit, as here in questions 4 and 7.

As you read through this section, you will discover that student A gains full marks for all the questions. This is so you can see what high-grade answers look like. The minimum for grade A is about 80% of the maximum mark (in this case around 80 marks). Student B makes many mistakes — often these are ones that examiners encounter frequently. I will tell you how many marks student B gets for each question and what sort of grade this mark represents. If the overall mark is about 40% of the total (around 40 marks), then student B will have passed at grade E standard. Use these benchmarks when trying the questions yourself.

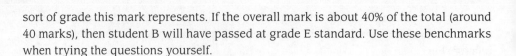

Examiner's comments

Each question part is followed by examiner comments (indicated by the icon e) that give tips on what you need to do to gain full marks. Students' answers are also followed by examiner's comments. These are preceded by the icon e and indicate where credit is due. In the weaker answers they also point out areas for improvement, specific problems and common errors, such as lack of clarity, weak or non-existent development of ideas or concepts, irrelevance, misinterpretation of the question and mistaken meanings of terms.

Question 1 **Biological molecules**

(a) Complete the table with a tick (✓) or a cross (✗) to indicate whether each of the statements about biological molecules applies to proteins, phospholipids, cellulose, glycogen and triglycerides.

	Hydrolysed to fatty acids	Present in plant cells	Molecule is a polymer	Contains nitrogen
Proteins				
Phospholipids				
Cellulose				
Glycogen				
Triglycerides				

(4 marks)

(b) Figure 1 shows a molecule of lactose, which is a disaccharide.

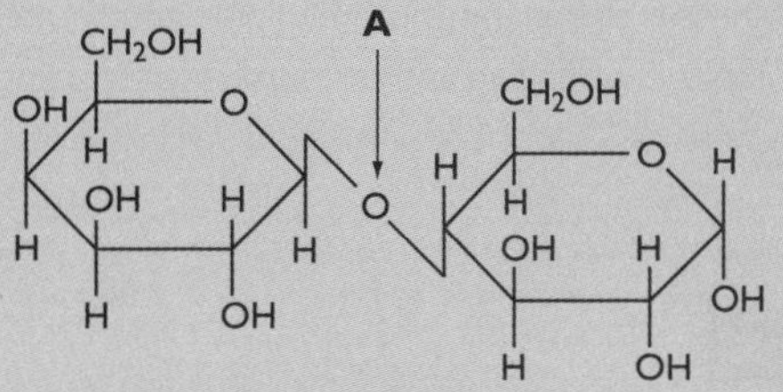

Figure 1

(i) Name the bond indicated by A on Figure 1. (1 mark)

ⓔ When asked to name, you have to give only a very brief answer. In this case one word is enough.

(ii) Draw an annotated diagram to show how the bond is broken. (3 marks)

ⓔ Annotated means you should add notes, not just give a diagram on its own.

Figure 2 is a ribbon model of a polypeptide showing its secondary and tertiary structure.

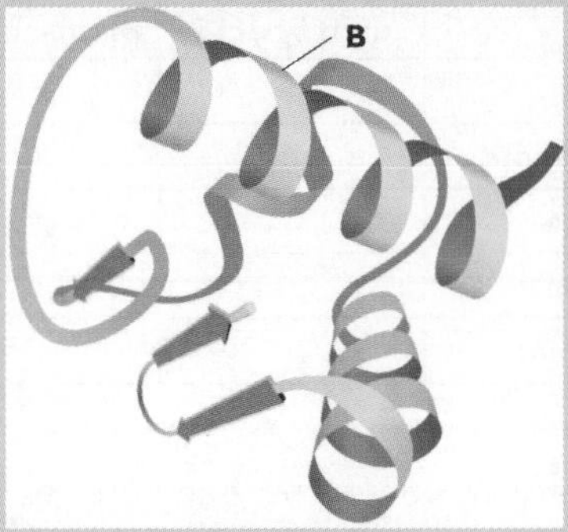

Figure 2

(c) State the name of the area labelled B on Figure 2. (1 mark)

ⓔ This is an example of a ribbon model of a protein. Make sure you have a look at these online so you get used to how they are depicted.

(d) Explain how the tertiary structure of polypeptides is stabilised. (4 marks)

ⓔ Notice that there are 4 marks for this question. That could be 1 mark for naming each bond or, more likely, 1 mark for naming each bond and explaining how it acts to stabilise tertiary structure.

(e) State *two* ways in which the *structure* of haemoglobin differs from the *structure* of the protein molecule shown in Figure 2. (2 marks)

ⓔ In a question like this, it is important that you state each difference clearly. For each point of difference state something about haemoglobin and something about the protein molecule shown in the figure. Before writing an answer recall what you know about the structure of haemoglobin. Points about function (transport of oxygen) will not gain any marks, even if true.

Total: 15 marks

Student A

(a)

	Hydrolysed to fatty acids	Present in plant cells	Molecule is a polymer	Contains nitrogen
Proteins	✗	✓	✓	✓
Phospholipids	✓	✓	✗	✓
Cellulose	✗	✓	✓	✗
Glycogen	✗	✗	✓	✗
Triglycerides	✓	✓	✗	✗

Student B

(a)

	Hydrolysed to fatty acids	Present in plant cells	Molecule is a polymer	Contains nitrogen
Proteins		✓	✓	✓
Phospholipids		✓	✓	✗
Cellulose		✓	✓	✓
Glycogen		✓	✓	✓
Triglycerides	✓		✓	✓

ⓔ Tick box questions look deceptively easy, but student B leaves blank spaces instead of putting in crosses. Always make sure you follow the instructions in the question. Student B also includes a tick with a line through it — a crossed tick. It is not clear to the examiner whether the candidate's answer is a tick or a cross so no mark will be awarded. If you change your mind about an answer, cross out your first answer completely and put in a new tick or cross. There are 4 marks, so you can be sure the examiner will give a mark for each column. In this case, student B does not score any marks. Notice where student B loses marks by comparing the two tables:

- forgetting that phospholipids have two fatty acids
- thinking that glycogen is stored in plants; starch (amylose and amylopectin) is the polysaccharide stored in plants
- thinking that all the macromolecules in the question are polymers; triglycerides and phospholipids are not polymers as they are not composed of sub-units joined together
- not knowing the elements found in the different biological molecules

Tables like the one in this question (and in the Content Guidance section of this book) are good ways to revise. You can make these tables part of your preparation for the examination.

Student A

(b) (i) Glycosidic

(ii)

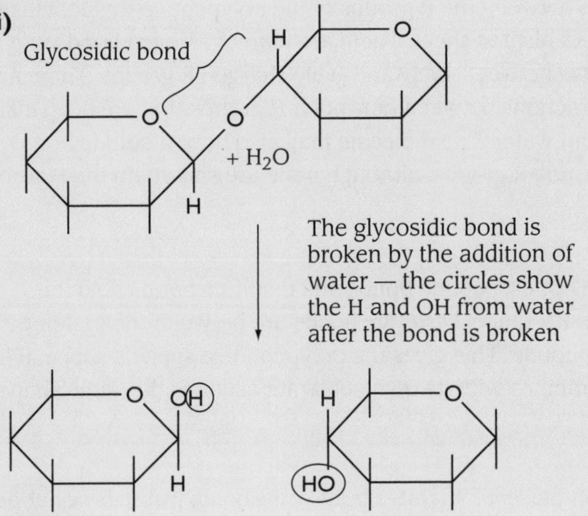

Student B

(b) (i) Glucosidic

(ii)

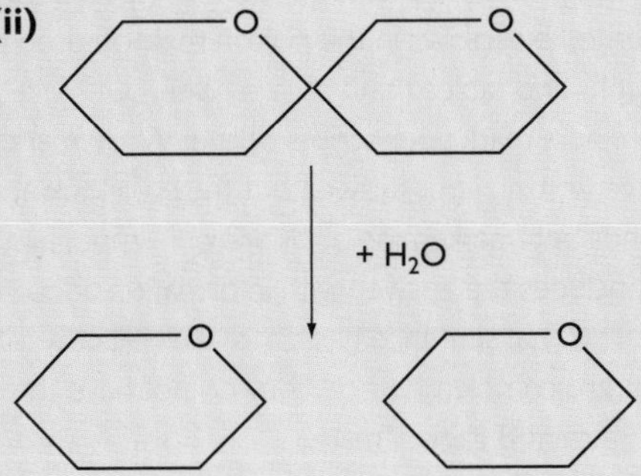

ⓔ The answers to (b)(i) show the importance of spelling technical terms correctly. Student B has written 'glucosidic' which would not be marked as correct. In part (ii), student B has forgotten to draw in the oxygen bridge between the two monosaccharide residues in lactose. This is a copying error from the question. student B has not added any notes to the diagram. Student B gains

1 mark for (b)(ii) as it is clear that water is used in the reaction. Note that student A has drawn the glycosidic bond slightly differently from the way it is shown in the question (Figure 1). Both are acceptable ways to show the bond in lactose.

Student A

(c) Alpha helix

Student B

(c) α helix

e Both students have the correct answer.

Student A

(d) There are many bonds between the R groups of the polypeptide that stabilise the alpha helix and the beta pleated sheet. There are many hydrogen bonds and ionic bonds. Ionic bonds form between +vely and –vely charged R groups. There are also hydrophobic interactions between non-polar R groups that are deep inside the molecule away from water. The molecule may also have disulfide bonds between sulfur-containing R groups, although none are shown on the Figure.

Student B

(d) Ionic bonds, hydrogen bonds, peptide bonds and disulfide bonds hold the polypeptide into a tertiary shape. Disulfide bonds are between the cysteine molecules in the polypeptide. This gives the polypeptide a specific shape. If it is an enzyme, then it combines with its own substrate as it has the same shape as the substrate.

e This is an 'explain' question. Student B has listed three of the bonds that stabilise polypeptides. In this question, it is likely that the examiner will only give marks for naming the correct bonds if there is some more information about each one. This means that student B gains a mark for giving correct information about disulfide bonds. Student A starts the answer well by referring to R groups. Student A could have labelled the alpha helix and beta-pleated sheets on Figure 2 to help the answer. The beta-pleated sheets are represented by arrows in the ribbon method used in the figure. You may write notes on diagrams, graphs and tables that you are given, but make sure that you always indicate this in your answer. Examiners mark your scripts online. While marking questions they only see the space where you have written your answer, but they will look at the whole page if you alert them to this. Peptide bonds between amino acids are only important in the primary structure of a polypeptide. Student B concludes the answer with information about the shape of the polypeptide, which is not required. The final sentence has a mistake — active sites of enzymes and their substrates have shapes that are complementary. They do not have the same shapes. If they did, they would not 'fit' together. Student B gains 1 mark.

Student A

(e) **(1)** Haemoglobin is made of four polypeptides, not just one.

(2) The polypeptide in the figure does not have a haem group.

Student B

(e) (1) It does not have haem.

(2) Haemoglobin is bigger.

ⓔ Student A makes it clear which of the two molecules is being described. The first answer given by B starts with 'it'. Examiners will often assume that candidates are referring to the first item when questions say 'state ways in which A differs from B'. Size is not a suitable answer to a question about structure. Student B gains 1 mark.

ⓔ **Student B gains 4 marks out of 15 for Question 1.**

Question 2 **Nucleic acids**

Figure 3 shows a small part of a molecule of DNA during replication.

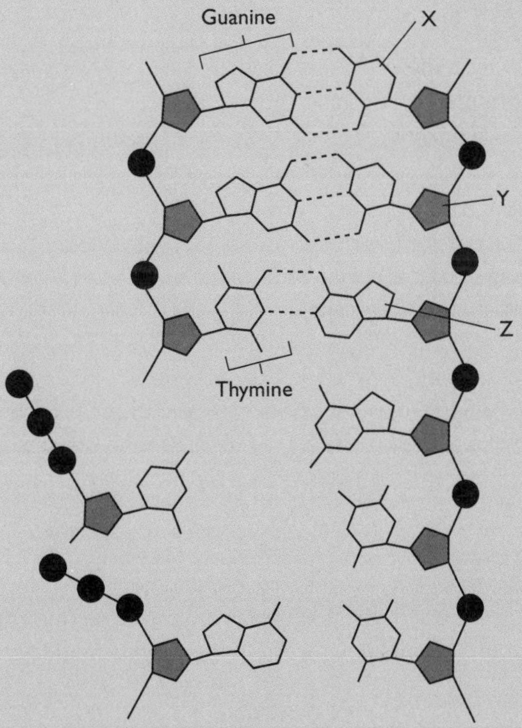

Figure 3

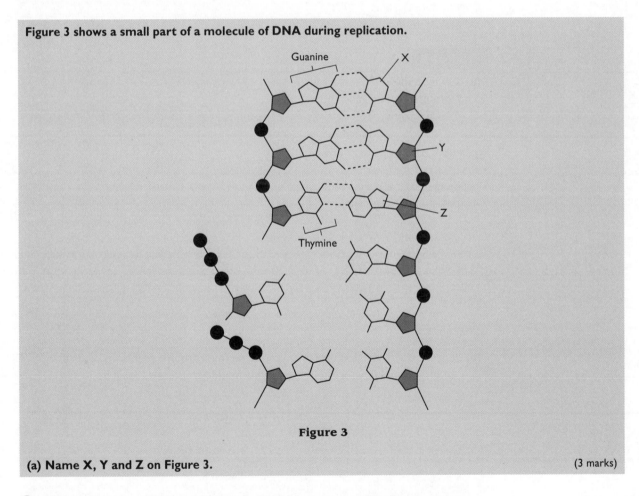

(a) Name X, Y and Z on Figure 3. (3 marks)

ⓔ When naming parts of DNA and RNA molecules take care over spelling. Examiners may insist on spelling being correct in cases where misspellings could indicate confusion with another compound. For example, the base thymine is often misspelt as 'thiamine', which is a vitamin.

(b) Using information in Figure 3, explain what is meant by the term *anti-parallel* when applied to DNA. (2 marks)

ⓔ Questions that start like this often give you some help in phrasing your answer. Study the figure carefully for information to use in the answer.

(c) Describe how DNA is replicated. You may refer to Figure 3 in your answer. (5 marks)

ⓔ Look carefully at the figure and use the information about the polynucleotides, their bases and base pairing to make the new molecule of DNA.

Total: 10 marks

Student A

(a) X — cytosine
Y — deoxyribose
Z — adenine

Student B

(a) X — cysteine
Y — sugar
Z — adenosine

ⓔ Student B has made three errors here:

- confusing cysteine (which is an amino acid) with cytosine
- not being specific about the name of the sugar in DNA
- misspelling adenine as adenosine

The 'backbone' of DNA is sometimes referred to as the sugar-phosphate backbone and you can use this expression when describing replication, for example. But here you should always be as specific as you can with the names you give. 'Sugar' could be a hexose (e.g. glucose), a pentose (e.g. ribose) or a disaccharide (e.g. sucrose). Pentose would be a slightly better answer, but that includes ribose, which is found in RNA and not DNA, so cannot be correct either. Student B gains no marks.

Student A

(b) Deoxyribose in the diagram is organised so that carbon 3 points upwards and carbon 5 points downward in the polynucleotide on the right, as here:

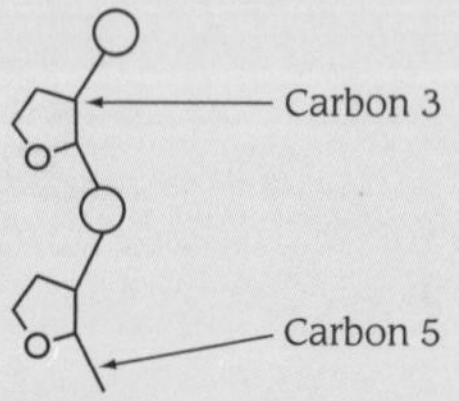

On the opposite polynucleotide sugar-phosphate backbone, the deoxyribose molecules are pointing in the opposite direction with carbon 3 at the bottom and carbon 5 at the top.

Student B

(b) The polynucleotides point in opposite directions.

ⓔ Student A has given a detailed answer realising that it is the orientation of the deoxyribose residues in the sugar-phosphate backbone that is the key point to make. The carbon atoms are numbered 1–5. Student B does not gain any marks as the detail expected is not here. This is unfortunate as he/she obviously knows what anti-parallel means. Make sure that you can define all the terms given in the learning outcomes of the OCR specification.

Student A

(c) The two polynucleotides separate as the hydrogen bonds between the bases are broken. Each polynucleotide acts as a template strand. DNA polymerase moves along each strand. As it moves along, free nucleotides are assembled against the template strands. In the example, a free nucleotide with a C is about to be paired with a G and a nucleotide with a T has just been paired with an A (Z on Figure 3). Two of the phosphates split away from the nucleotide providing energy for the formation of a phosphodiester bond between sugar (deoxyribose) and phosphate.

Student B

(c) The strands separate and one strand acts as a template for making another new strand. Bases are matched together by base pairing and these are joined together to make a new strand.

ⓔ Student A has easily gained the 5 marks for this question and has made good use of the material in the figure, as recommended by the examiner. Student B has not stated that both polynucleotides act as templates, has not used the information in the figure and has not used appropriate terminology. Student B gains no marks even though base pairing has been mentioned — the examiner would expect information from the figure to be used before awarding a mark.

ⓔ **Student B gains 0 marks out of 10 for Question 2.**

Question 3 **Enzymes**

A student investigated the effect of increasing enzyme concentration on the activity of a protease. Milk protein was used as the substrate. Different concentrations of the enzyme were made up as shown in Table 1. 2 cm^3 of each protease solution was added to 10 cm^3 of the milk solution and the time taken for the cloudiness to disappear was recorded. The investigation was carried out at 35°C.

The rate of reaction was calculated as 1000/t, where t = time taken for disappearance of the cloudiness. The student's results are shown in Table 1.

Table 1

Concentration of protease/$g\,dm^{-3}$	Time taken for cloudiness to disappear/s	Rate of reaction $(1000/t)/s^{-1}$
0.0	No change	0.0
1.0	555	1.8
2.5	166	6.0
5.0	92	10.9
7.5	73	13.7
10.0	49	

(a) (i) Calculate the rate of reaction when the concentration of the enzyme was 10 $g\,dm^{-3}$. Show your working. (2 marks)

Always check the way you carry out a calculation using already-calculated numbers to make sure you have the right method.

(ii) Describe and explain the results. Use the data in the table to illustrate your answer. (5 marks)

Even if the question does not advise you to use the data, you should always do this when describing results.

(b) State *two* factors that would be kept constant and state how the student would keep them constant in this investigation. (4 marks)

Remember the four factors that influence enzyme activity. One is the independent variable, so you have a choice of two from three.

(c) Explain how the student could use a colorimeter to follow the course of each reaction to find the *initial* rate of reaction. (3 marks)

You should know about using a colorimeter from the Benedict's test (see page 20). This question is asking you to apply your knowledge to a new situation — there will be quite a few such questions in the examination.

Salivary amylase catalyses the hydrolysis of starch to maltose. It is claimed that calcium and chloride ions are required as cofactors by salivary amylase.

(d) Explain how the student would investigate the claim that calcium and chloride ions are cofactors for salivary amylase. In your answer you should make clear the sequence of steps in the investigation. (8 marks)

This question asks for a plan for this investigation. The best way to show the sequence of steps is to write a list of numbered points.

Total: 22 marks

Student A

(a) (i) 1000/49 = 20.4 s^{-1}

(ii) The rate at which the milk protein is broken down increases as the concentration of the enzyme increases. The rate at 10.0 g dm^{-3} (20.4 s^{-1}) is double that at 5.0 g dm^{-3} (10.9 s^{-1}). The cloudiness disappears because the milk protein is hydrolysed by the protease breaking the peptide bonds between the amino acids. As the concentration of enzyme increases, there are more active sites available and there are more collisions between protease molecules and the milk protein molecules. More enzyme–substrate complexes can form.

Student B

(a) (i) 20.4 s^{-1}

(ii) There is a direct relationship between rate and concentration of enzyme. When there is no enzyme, there can be no reaction (or the rate is so slow that it cannot be measured) as there are no active sites available. As more enzyme is available, there are more active sites for the substrate molecules, so the rate increases.

e Both students have the correct answer for the calculation. Student B has not followed the instruction to give the working, but examiners will often give full marks even if working is not shown. However, it is always safe to write down the calculation as student A has done because you may make a mistake and the examiner can give 1 mark if you show the correct working. Note that both students have expressed the answer to one decimal place to match the other rates given in the table. They will have rounded down from 20.41 to 20.4. The examiner may ask you to put the answer in the table. Always look for this instruction and follow it. In part (ii), student A has given a description of the results and illustrated it with a comparative data quote. The candidate has gone on to explain why the cloudiness has disappeared and explained why the rate increases as there is an increase in concentration of enzyme. Student B has said that there is a 'direct relationship' without saying what that is. It may help to sketch a graph to see the relationship when you are asked to describe what is shown in a table. The student has not developed the answer to explain the effect of an increase in active sites. Student B would gain 1 mark for referring correctly to active sites. He/she has not used any data so has not gained an easy mark here. When you are describing data in graphs or tables, always include a data quote to illustrate what you are describing. Often data quotes should be comparative, e.g. the rate increased from X to Y as the enzyme concentration was increased from A to B. Don't forget to use the units when giving data quotes.

Student A

(b) pH. The student would use a buffer solution at a set pH, perhaps the optimum pH for the enzyme.

Temperature. The test-tubes would be placed into a thermostatically controlled water bath at a set temperature — perhaps the enzyme's optimum temperature.

Student B

(b) Concentration of enzyme. The amount of the enzyme added to each test-tube must be the same.

Concentration of milk. The amount of milk added to each test-tube must be the same.

e Student A gives a thorough answer. You should know that buffer solutions are used to control the pH. It would also be a good idea to use a pH meter to check that the target pH is achieved in each test tube. Note how the student controls temperature. Just saying 'use a water bath' is not enough. A water bath could be a beaker with water and a thermometer. It is possible to keep the temperature reasonably constant by heating with a Bunsen burner or adding hot and cold water, but it is time consuming and difficult to achieve a constant temperature. Using a water bath with a thermostat, heater and thermometer means that all you need to do is check the thermometer from time to time to make sure the water bath is working properly. Always refer to these water baths as thermostatically controlled water baths. Student B shows some confusion. The first answer is the independent variable in this investigation and is changed each time rather than being kept the same throughout. The student gains no marks for this. In the second answer there is confusion over the use of the word 'amount'. The concentration of the milk protein is a variable that must be controlled, so the student has 1 mark for stating the variable, but 'amount' here could mean concentration (mass of milk powder per unit volume of water) or it could mean the volume of milk solution added. Both of these answers would be correct, but the student has not given a clear answer, so does not gain a second mark.

Student A

(c) $10\,cm^3$ of the milk solution with $2\,cm^3$ of distilled water could be put into a colorimeter and a reading taken for absorbance. This is equivalent to the very start of the reaction just as the enzyme is added (time = 0 seconds). The first enzyme solution ($1\,g\,dm^{-3}$) is added to the milk solution and immediately put into the colorimeter. The absorbance readings are taken every 10 seconds. This is repeated with fresh milk solutions and the other enzyme concentrations as in the table. This would be done at room temperature rather than 35°C, so the rate would be slower than in the table. A graph is drawn and the initial rate is calculated by taking the tangent as shown here:

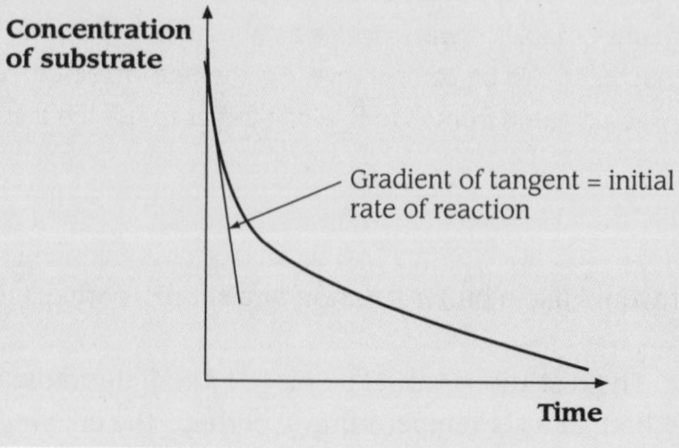

Student B

(c) When the milk and enzyme solution are mixed, the cloudiness disappears. It is difficult to tell exactly when the cloudiness has disappeared, so the student could put the test tube into a colorimeter and wait until the reading is 0. The student can then record the time taken to reach a reading of 0 in the colorimeter and this will be a better measurement of the rate of the reaction than just looking at it with your eyes. People will differ in the way in which they see the cloudiness and they may not always get the same result when looking at the same test tube.

e Student A has given a full answer. Unfortunately, student B has not understood the question and does not gain any marks. The examiner has not asked the candidates to improve the way in which the results of the student's investigation are taken — which is the question that student B has answered. To find the initial rate, readings have to be taken at frequent intervals and plotted on a graph, as student A describes. Calculating $1000/t$ (t = time taken for milk solution to clear) as the rate of the reaction is fine, but it does not give you the rate at the very beginning when substrate concentration is not limiting. Another way to use the colorimeter is to connect it to a data logger and computer. The software will plot a graph to show the decrease in absorbance with time. It is possible to put test-tubes into some colorimeters. With others, the reaction mixtures are placed into cuvettes, which are transparent, plastic containers square in cross section.

The graph on the opposite page shows the concentration of substrate. This is determined by using the colorimeter to take absorbance readings for different dilutions of the milk solution. The results are used to draw a graph that is used to convert absorbance readings into concentrations of substrate.

Student A

(d) The student should use a 1% starch solution and collect some salivary amylase. The same volume of starch solution should be put into each of three test tubes and the same volume of a buffer solution (e.g. pH 7) should be added to each tube to keep the pH the same in each tube. Calcium chloride solution is added to each tube. Another three tubes can be set up with no calcium chloride. Instead, to keep the volume the same in these control tubes, the student should add exactly the same volume of distilled water. The tubes can be put in a thermostatically controlled water bath at 37°C (body temperature). The same volume of salivary amylase is added to each tube. Samples can be taken from the test tubes every 30 seconds, iodine solution added and put in a colorimeter and a reading for absorbance taken. If calcium and chloride ions are required as cofactors by the enzyme, then the colour of the iodine solution will gradually become lighter so that the absorbance readings decrease in the tubes with calcium chloride. The iodine solution will be blue-black each time with samples taken from the control tubes and the absorbance reading will be high and not change. If calcium and chloride ions are *not* required, then both sets of tubes will show starch digestion.

Student B

(d) The student should set up five test tubes with the same concentration of starch. These should be put in a water bath so that they are all at the same temperature. Some salivary amylase should be put into a beaker and kept at the same temperature. Then some chloride ions will be put into the first test-tube (A) followed by some of the salivary amylase. The student then adds iodine and waits to see how long it takes for the blue-black colour to disappear. The rate can then be calculated as $1/t$. This is repeated with all the other tubes (B to E) but each time add slightly more of the chloride ions, so the amount of chloride ions increases. Then plot a graph of concentration of chloride ions against the rate of reaction ($1/t$).

e Student A has used some of the techniques given earlier in the question when preparing this answer. It is always a good idea to look back to earlier part questions when you come to write a long-answer question like this. Notice how precise the answer is. The answer does show the sequence of steps, so gains the mark for quality of written communication. The student has not told us what volumes to use, but we are told to use the same volume in each case. We are also told that the total volume in the tubes should be the same. This is something that student B has not done. Notice that all student B's tubes will contain chloride ions — there is no mention of calcium ions, which should be included. There needs to be a tube without calcium and chloride ions to see if salivary amylase will catalyse the hydrolysis of starch without the cofactors. Student B has increased the concentration of the chloride ions (which is not necessary) so it is possible that the rate of this enzyme-catalysed reaction will increase. But the concentration in the first tube (A) might provide more than enough of the cofactor for all the enzyme molecules to function at their maximum rate for this temperature. Student B makes a number of other mistakes:

- the temperature is not specified; this is a human enzyme so a temperature near to 37°C would be appropriate, although sometimes the reaction might be too fast and a lower temperature would be used
- the concentration of starch is not given
- the volume of salivary amylase is not given — at least the answer should say 'use the same volume of salivary amylase in each tube'
- it is not possible to add 'chloride ions'; note that student A has used a solution of calcium chloride which provides both required ions
- referring to iodine solution as 'iodine'
- the disappearance of starch cannot be followed by adding iodine solution as it inhibits the action of amylase
- when describing how to draw a graph always write 'draw a graph of the dependent variable against the independent variable'; in student B's investigation that would be 'draw a graph of the rate of starch breakdown against the concentration of chloride ions'

It would be difficult to calculate the concentration of chloride ions because each tube has a different total volume; always make sure that the volume in the reaction mixtures is the same — as A did by adding distilled water.

Student B gains 1 mark for stating that temperature is controlled. The sequence of steps is not shown well, so student B does not gain the mark for quality of written communication.

Note that there are some safety issues with the student's investigation. Some schools and colleges have policies that preclude students using their own saliva in science practicals. There are other amylases that can be used, but they are not quite the same and may not rely on calcium and chloride ions as cofactors.

There are good websites for A-level chemists that have information on biochemistry and the topic is covered in some A-level chemistry textbooks. See: **www.chemguide.co.uk** and **www.chemistry-react.org**. In both cases, you will have to search for biochemistry topics, such as proteins and DNA, but you will find much helpful material if you want to know more or deepen your understanding.

e **Student B gains 4 marks out of 22 for Question 3.**

Question 4 **Diet and food production**

The body mass index (BMI) is calculated using the following formula:

$$\mathbf{BMI} = \frac{\textbf{body mass in kg}}{\textbf{height in metres}^2}$$

Table 2 shows the categories for BMI.

Table 2

BMI	Category
Below 20	Underweight
20–25	Acceptable
25–30	Overweight
Over 30	Obese
Over 40	Very obese

(a) Complete Table 3 below by:

(i) calculating the BMI for person C

(ii) using Table 2 to identify the appropriate category for this person

Table 3

Person	Height/m	Mass/kg	BMI	Category
A	1.60	60	23	Acceptable
B	1.65	48	18	Underweight
C	1.50	74		

(2 marks)

e This question is as simple as shown. There are always easy questions on the exam papers. Do not throw away the marks by looking for something complicated.

(b) Random samples of people are chosen to take part in health surveys. These people are weighed and measured; their BMI is calculated and they are recorded in one of the four categories given in Table 2. Table 4 shows results for men and women who took part in these health surveys between 1980 and 2006. The total number of men and women in each sample was 1000.

Table 4

BMI category	Year					
Men	**1980**	**1986**	**1993**	**1999**	**2001**	**2006**
Below 20	100	60	50	40	40	10
20–25	510	490	390	330	280	320
25–30	330	380	430	440	470	430
Over 30	60	70	130	190	210	240
Women						
Below 20	140	110	80	70	60	200
20–25	540	530	460	390	380	420
25–30	240	240	300	330	330	340
Over 30	80	120	160	210	230	240

(i) Calculate the percentage change in the number of men who have a BMI over 30 between 1980 and 2006. Show your working. (2 marks)

e Calculation of percentage change is a common exam question. Make sure you know how to carry out such calculations.

(ii) Suggest why health authorities in countries such as the UK are concerned about the increasing numbers of people who are obese and very obese. (4 marks)

e This sort of question looks deceptively easy. You need to make four good points. It is best if they are about different aspects of the impact of increasing numbers of obese people. Notice the question says 'health authorities' so restrict your answer to the consequences of obesity on health.

(c) There is a rising demand for food in the world. Some farmers now concentrate on growing biofuels. Farmers use a variety of techniques to ensure high yields. As a result the world's biodiversity is under threat.

Discuss the threats to biodiversity as a result of increased demand for food and biofuels.

In your answer, you should make clear the effects of the threats you discuss. (8 marks)

e This question requires a lengthy answer. Go through the question carefully and circle or underline the different parts to the question. Make sure you discuss both the increased demand for food and the growing of biofuels.

Total: 16 marks

Student A

(a) 33; obese

Student B

(a) 49; very obese

ⓔ When calculating the BMI, it is necessary to take the square of the height. Student B has forgotten to do this. The examiner would carry forward an error here and award 1 mark for choosing the appropriate category for the answer that has been calculated.

Student A

(b) (i) (240 – 60)/60 × 100 = 300%

Student B

(b) (i) 60/240 × 100 = 25%

ⓔ Calculating percentage changes is not the same thing as calculating a simple percentage. You are calculating the difference in the figures and then expressing that as a percentage of the original figure. Student B has calculated the original figure (60) as a percentage of the final figure, which is incorrect and so gains no marks. Remember this formula:

percentage change = difference/original × 100%

Student A

(b) (ii) Obesity is a risk factor in many diseases, such as diabetes, cancer, heart disease and arthritis. This means that obese people require treatment for many different conditions and these are expensive and a drain on resources of the NHS. Also, people who have these health conditions may take time off work and so do not contribute as much to the economy and may need disability payments. They may also find it difficult to move about and need special help such as wheelchairs, which may be provided by the government. The table shows that numbers of people with obesity are rising sharply and are not reaching a peak.

Student B

(b) (ii) People who are obese and very obese probably will develop heart conditions like CHD and atherosclerosis. The fat in their bloodstream gets deposited in their blood vessels and blocks them. They get pains in their chest, cannot move about easily and may have heart attacks.

ⓔ In this type of question it is best to make a number of different points and keep looking at the question to make sure you are answering it. It is a 'Suggest' question, so there are likely to be many different points that candidates could make and that the examiners will accept. Student A identifies the diseases linked to obesity and explains the likely effect on the NHS and the economy. You are expected, as part of your course, to appreciate social and economic aspects such as this. Student B has linked CHD to obesity and gains a mark, although it is not a good idea to write '...will develop

CHD', but to write 'they are at greater risk of developing' or use the phrase 'risk factor', as student A has done. Student B then deals with how CHD develops, which is not relevant to the question. Also note that when describing atherosclerosis you should refer to deposits in the walls of arteries. Plaque will not block an artery, but will reduce the width of the lumen and increase the chances of a blood clot that could block the artery. This answer needs more development and only gains 1 mark.

Student A

(c) Increasing demand for food and biofuels means that farmers need more land to grow crops and keep animals. This means that ecosystems like rainforest are cut down and therefore habitats for many organisms are destroyed. The land is used to grow crops like soya beans and oil palms as monocultures, which do not have much biodiversity as they do not provide many different habitats. To control pests and diseases, farmers use chemical pesticides, which often kill harmless, non-target species, so reducing biodiversity. Chemical fertilisers are used to increase yields, but often they run off into rivers and cause eutrophication which reduces the number of species. Some places have been overgrazed so there is very little vegetation to support primary consumers; this leads to erosion, which degrades the land. Some types of fishing, like trawling, damage the bottom of the sea. In many parts of the North Sea there are no natural ecosystems left. Removal of many fish damages food webs and when stocks (e.g. of cod) are exhausted, fishermen take animals lower down the food chain (e.g. sand eels). This has an effect on organisms like puffins, which feed on sand eels, and their numbers decrease. Biodiversity includes the number of organisms of different species.

Student B

(c) Many farmers spray their crops with chemicals, like DDT. This kills many species, both those that they want to kill and those that may be good, such as predators of pests. Herbicides kill weeds but spray drift may mean that they also kill plants around the fields (say in hedgerows) where wild plants grow. This reduces the biodiversity of plant life, including plants that are food for caterpillars and other animals. To grow crops that give high yields, farmers apply fertilisers, which damage the environment. More food means that natural habitats, like rainforests, are cut down, so this means biodiversity is lost. It is important to maintain biodiversity because we may need the genes and alleles in the wild plants that are related to crop plants to improve those crops in the future.

e This is another question requiring an answer that deals with different ideas. Student A has ranged over habitat loss, monocultures, pesticides, fertilisers and land degradation without forgetting that food is harvested from the wild. The answer looks as if the student has read around the subject and knows about the terrible effects of over-fishing. Student B gains 1 mark for the point made about killing predators of pests and 2 marks for the points made about herbicides. The point about fertilisers is too general — 'damage the environment' — and does not answer the question, which is about biodiversity. This means that the student would not gain the mark for quality of written communication. Student B also makes a point about habitat destruction, but then explains why it is important to maintain biodiversity for the future of agriculture. This is not asked in the question. Student B gets 4 marks. Mark schemes for this sort of question are likely to have a few marks available for each of the topics that the examiners expect to find. So do not write at length about one or two reasons — think of several different ones. It is also a good idea to plan your answer. You can do this by writing topic headings at intervals down the left-hand side of the page on the examination paper. This will make sure you write several points about a range of topics rather than concentrating on just a few. Spend a few minutes planning out your answer before you start writing it.

e Student B gets 6 marks out of 16 for Question 4.

Question 5 **Health and disease**

Tuberculosis (TB) is caused by the bacterial pathogen *Mycobacterium tuberculosis*.

(a) Describe how *M. tuberculosis* is transmitted. (2 marks)

e Transmission is the passage of a pathogen from an infected to an uninfected person. When describing transmission make sure you refer to exit of the pathogen from the infected person and entry into the non-infected person.

(b) Figure 4 shows the number of notified cases of tuberculosis from 1913 to 2006 in England and Wales.

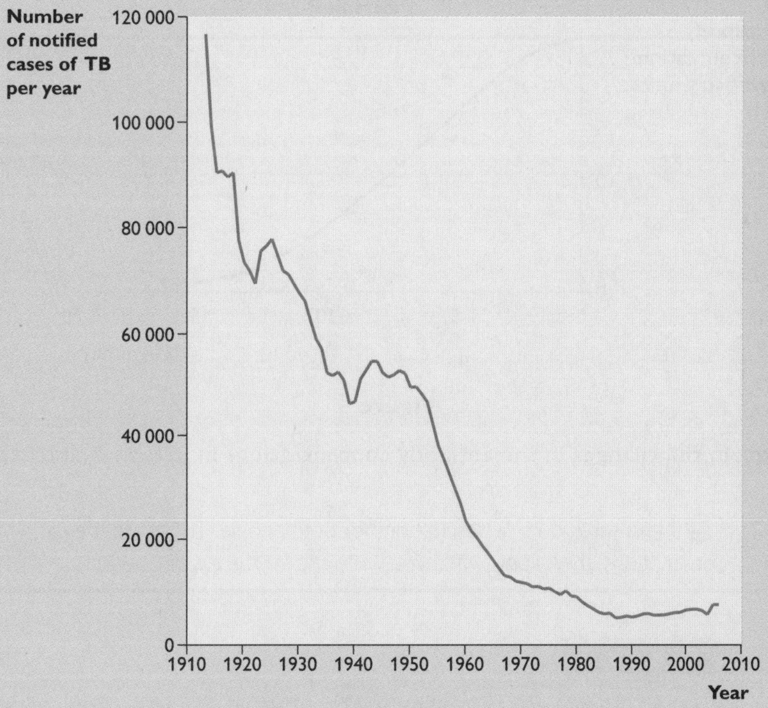

Figure 4

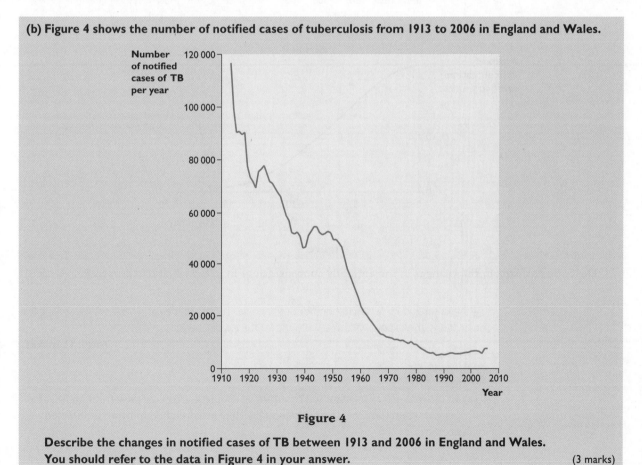

Describe the changes in notified cases of TB between 1913 and 2006 in England and Wales. You should refer to the data in Figure 4 in your answer. (3 marks)

Ⓔ Use a ruler to follow the changes. Position the ruler vertically against the *y*-axis and move it slowly across the graph. Rule lines at places where there is a significant change in the trend. Use your ruled vertical lines to help you to give accurate data quotes. Do not forget to use units.

(c) Tetanus is caused by another bacterial pathogen, *Clostridium tetani*. In an investigation of the effectiveness of active and passive immunity, person A was given a vaccine against tetanus. Person P was given some antibodies against tetanus. The concentration of anti-tetanus antibodies in the blood of both people was monitored over the next few weeks. The results are shown in Figure 5.

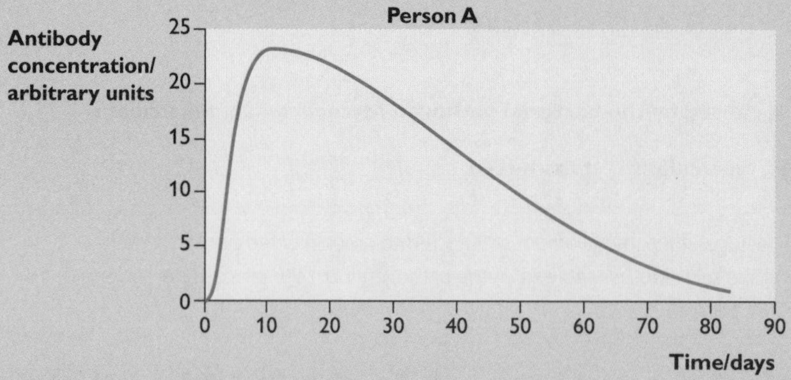

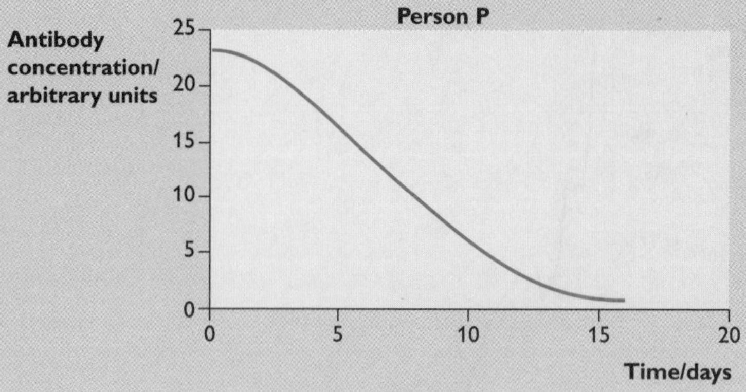

Figure 5

Describe *and* explain the changes in the antibody concentrations in person A and in person P. (6 marks)

Ⓔ Make sure you give descriptions for both people. Those are the easy marks. While writing the descriptions, think about what you will write for the explanations.

Total: 11 marks

Student A

(a) *M. tuberculosis* is transmitted by airborne droplets. Droplets pass from an infected person when they breathe out or cough. They are breathed in by an uninfected person.

Student B

(a) TB is transmitted in the air in droplets.

e The examiner is likely to give marks for describing how *Mycobacterium tuberculosis* leaves the infected person and enters the uninfected person. So when you describe disease transmission for any of the three diseases in the specification always make sure that you state how the pathogen leaves the infected person and how it enters the uninfected person. It is a good idea to use these two words in your answer. Student B has not, so does not gain a mark.

Student A

(b) The number of notified cases of TB decreased significantly between 1913 and 2006. The percentage decrease was about 95% from about 110000 to about 7000. But in the early 1920s and in the 1940s the numbers increased. There was a sharp decrease after the 1950s, but the numbers increased slightly after 1990.

Student B

(b) The number of cases went down from about 110000 in 1913 to 90000 in 1915 when it levelled out a bit and then increased. This was during the First World War. Then the numbers decreased until 1922 when they increased from 50000 to 78000. They then fell until 1940, when they increased because of the Second World War. After that the numbers fell dramatically.

e Student A has started the answer by stating something very obvious, but there are often marks for this, so make sure that you write the simple things first. The question prompts the candidates to use data and both of these answers have. Student A has calculated a percentage change from the data, which is an excellent idea. Student B has given several data quotes, but to gain marks each data quote should include a year and the number of cases. The date corresponding to 78000 should be given in the answer. When you are given a graph without grid lines (as in Figure 4), you do not have to give precise data quotes — e.g. 'about 11 000' is fine. However, you should be quite close and it is best to use a ruler to draw intercepts on the figure to make sure that you are as precise as you can be. If there are gridlines on the graph, then you have to read the figures from the graph accurately. Student B has stated 50000 for 1922 when the figure is nearer 70000. You can also annotate the graph with lines and labels and refer to different sections. This graph could also be divided into several sections. But do not overdo this, as there are only 3 marks available. Do not take too long over a question with few marks. Notice also that Student B explains that the increases occurred during the two World Wars. The question does not ask for an explanation. Student B gains 2 marks for conveying the general trend and giving a data quote for the years 1913 to 1915.

Student A

(c) Person A: the antibody concentration increases very steeply soon after the vaccination was given to 23 au by day 10. This is a secondary immune response, so the person had already been vaccinated against tetanus. B memory cells responded and changed into plasma cells, which released antibodies. The plasma cells remain in the body releasing antibodies for some time which is why the antibody concentration remains higher for longer compared with passive immunity. Person P: antibodies were injected so the concentration was high immediately. They decreased because they are not being produced by plasma cells and will gradually be destroyed. A shows active immunity and P shows passive immunity.

Student B

(c) After the vaccine was given, the amount of antibodies went up and stayed quite high. In passive immunity, the antibodies are injected straight into the bloodstream and they remove the pathogens. This is why the concentration is high to begin with (at time 0). The antibodies combine with the pathogen and make it easier for white blood cells to carry out phagocytosis. They also cause them to clump together (agglutination), which helps phagocytosis. They may also combine with viruses to prevent them entering cells and they combine with toxins to neutralise them. In active immunity, only B cells specific to *Clostridium tetani* respond to release antibodies. It takes time and they secrete antibodies into the blood which is why the concentration starts near 0 and goes up.

e Student B has not given a good description of the data: 'went up and stayed quite high' is not precise enough and there is no description of the change in P. No data have been used. Student B has explained what happens in active and passive immunity to give the different shapes shown in the graphs, although there is no reference to memory cells. Then there is an answer to another question: 'explain how antibodies function to protect the body against pathogens'. Student B gains 2 marks. Student A has given a data quote and described the changes to the antibody concentration. The abbreviation 'au' is acceptable here. The answer also includes information about the secondary immune response. This is very good, because the student has spotted that the antibody concentration increased almost immediately. If person A had not been vaccinated beforehand there would have been a longer gap before the antibody concentration increased.

e **Student B gets 4 marks out of 11 for Question 5.**

Question 6 **Biodiversity**

Some students studied the biodiversity of animals on chalk downland and greensand heath in 10 randomly placed quadrats. To assess the biodiversity they calculated Simpson's index of diversity (*D*). Table 5 shows their results.

Table 5

	Chalk downland			Greensand heath		
Animals	**Number of animals in sample**	**Number of individuals of each animal (*n*) ÷ total number of animals (*N*)**	**$(n/N)^2$**	**Number of animals in sample**	**Number of individuals of each animal (*n*) ÷ total number of animals (*N*)**	**$(n/N)^2$**
Snails	147	0.2097	0.04397	0	0	0
Mites	9	0.0128	0.00016	17	0.0556	0.00309
Flies	21	0.0300	0.00090	15	0.0490	0.00240
Grasshoppers	5	0.0071	0.00005	0	0	0
Springtails	25	0.0357	0.00127	3	0.010	0.00010
Millipedes	37	0.0528	0.00279	0	0	0
Centipedes	38	0.0542	0.00294	1	0.0033	0.00001
Earwigs	12	0.0171	0.00029	0	0	0
Beetles	49	0.0699	0.00489	62	0.2026	0.04105
Butterflies	2	0.0029	0.00001	11	0.0359	0.00129
Earthworms	46	0.0656	0.00431	0	0	0
Woodlice	218	0.3110	0.09671	8	0.0261	0.00068
True bugs	4	0.0057	0.00003	74	0.2418	0.05848
Spiders	88	0.1255	0.01576	115	0.3758	0.14124
Totals	**701**		**0.17408**	**306**		**0.24834**
Index of diversity (*D*)	0.83					

(Source: Lewis, T. and Taylor, L. R. (1967) *Introduction to Experimental Ecology*, Academic Press)

The formula for calculating Simpson's index of diversity (*D*) is:

$$D = 1 - (\Sigma(n/N)^2)$$

where *N* = the total number of animals found and *n* is the number of individuals of a particular group.

(a) Complete the table by calculating Simpson's index of diversity for the greensand heath. (1 mark)

e Do not forget to take a calculator to the exam. You are not allowed to use your mobile phone for calculations!

(b) Explain how the students would be sure that they had collected random samples. (2 marks)

e The clue to the answer is in the question: 'ten randomly placed quadrats'. Explain how the students placed their quadrats randomly. Remember it is best to mark out an area of ground with tapes when doing this type of exercise.

(c) Make one criticism of the assessment of biodiversity in this study. (1 mark)

e Look carefully at the question for help with deciding on a criticism to make.

(d) Springtails are small animals (less than 6 mm in length) that are found in very large numbers in soils and leaf litter. They are important in ecosystems as detritivores that eat dead plant material, so contributing to the recycling of materials. A study was carried out on the abundance and habitat preference of two species of springtail, *Friesea mirabilis* and *Friesia truncata*, in three woodlands in Norway. The woodlands were dominated by birch, *Betula pubescens*, Norway spruce, *Picea abies*, and sitka spruce, *Picea sitchensis* and *P. lutzi*.

Figure 6 shows the abundance of the two species of springtail in soils in the three woodlands in June and October 2004.

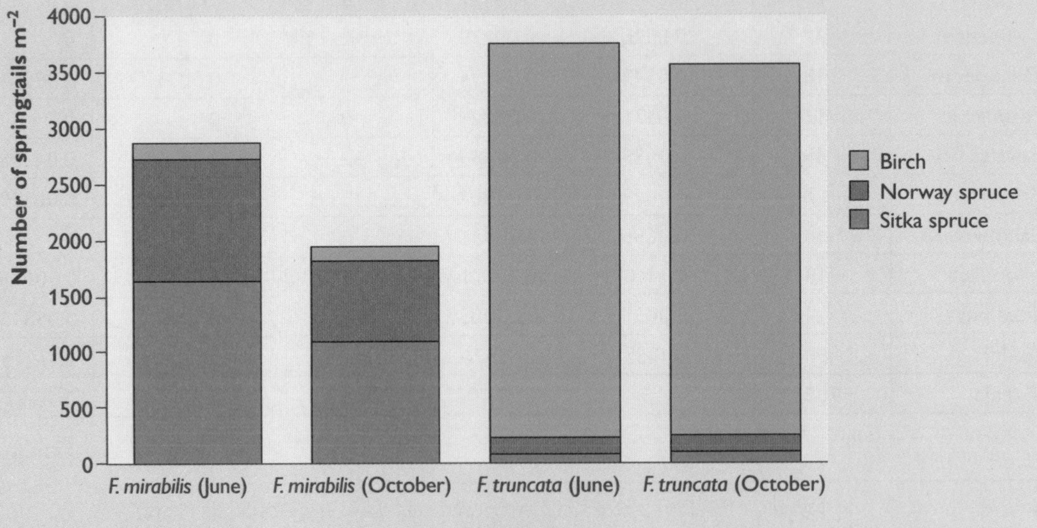

Figure 6

Summarise the evidence given in Figure 6 about the abundance and habitat preferences of the two species of springtail. (6 marks)

e You do not know the answer to this question, so you will have to spend time analysing and interpreting the data in the figure. You should make notes on the exam paper and annotate the figure to sort out what you are going to write.

Total: 10 marks

Student A

(a) 0.75

Student B

(a) 0.25

ⓔ Student B has forgotten to subtract 0.25 from 1 in order to give the Simpson's index of diversity. As there is only 1 mark for this, student B does not score.

Student A

(b) They could make a grid by laying out two tape measures at right angles to each other. Then they use a program to generate random numbers, which are the coordinates for putting down the quadrats.

Student B

(b) Put two ropes down on the ground to make two sides of a square. Look up random numbers in a random number table. If the first number is 1006, walk ten paces along one of the ropes and then 6 paces in the direction of the other rope. When you stop, put down the quadrat. Repeat this for other random numbers.

ⓔ Both students have explained how to position a quadrat randomly within a square delimited by tape measures or ropes. Student B gains 2 marks.

Student A

(c) The students did not identify the organisms to the species level, only to a higher taxonomic level. Spiders, for example are a group of arthropods. The data does not tell us how many species are present. There could be just one species in each group in one forest and lots of species in the groups in the other.

Student B

(c) There are other organisms in the soil: fungi and bacteria. The students have not identified them.

ⓔ Both students score the mark here as they each make a valid criticism. It would be very difficult to identify the soil organisms to the level of species; this would take an expert's knowledge. In many surveys of biodiversity, the list of organisms contains both individual species and higher taxonomic groups, such as families and orders. It would also be impossible to identify the soil bacteria and fungi without taking samples and growing them on agar. This would take a long time. However, both students are correct in that if we are to assess the biodiversity of an area we should take account of all the species from all three domains. They could also mention that some animals are only active at night and would not be caught during the day and that there are likely to be seasonal changes in the species present.

Student A

(d) *F. truncata* is more abundant in the birch forest than in the other forests in both June and October. It seems to prefer this habitat as there are very few of them in the sitka spruce and the Norway spruce forests (less than 270 m^{-2}) whereas there are over 3000 m^{-2} in birch. *F. mirabilis* prefers sitka spruce as there are more of them in both June and October compared with the other forests (>1500 m^{-2} in June compared with about 1000 m^{-2} in Norway spruce and about 150 m^{-2} in birch). *F. mirabilis* does not appear to like birch as the numbers are about 150 m^{-2} in both months. The numbers of *F. mirabilis* decrease by about a third in October compared with June. The decrease in numbers of *F. truncata* in October is much smaller and may not be significant but a sampling error.

Student B

(d) There are more springtails of the *Friesia truncata* species than the other species in June and October. This may be because they can feed on birch, but not on spruce. Most of this species live on the birch trees whereas few live on the other trees. *Friesia mirabilis* prefers the spruce trees as a habitat as very few were found on the birch trees. There may be a slight preference for sitka spruce.

e This question is an exercise in translating data from one form into another. As there are 6 marks available, it is a good idea to annotate the bar chart before starting to write your answer. This will help you identify at least six things to write. As in Question 5 (b) you should start with something obvious. Also, make sure that you use the data to support the statements that you make, as student A has done. Student B's first statement does not really make much sense. The total number of springtails is for three different forests. It would be better to say that the highest abundance (or density) is of *F. truncata* in birch forests. Student B has not used any data and only gains 2 marks for the statements made. The springtails live in the soils not on the trees.

e **Student B gets 5 marks out of 10 for Question 6.**

Question 7 **Classification and evolution**

(a) Define the term *phylogeny*. **(1 mark)**

e Remember to learn definitions of all the terms used in the learning outcomes in the specification.

Taxonomists use a great variety of different features of organisms when devising classification systems. Recently, DNA barcoding has been suggested as a way to distinguish between different species of plants, animals and micro-organisms. Barcoding involves sequencing the DNA from certain genes in groups of organisms. It has been used to show that there are eleven distinct groups of giraffe in Africa and to help separate species of butterfly that appear similar but do

not reproduce with each other. Studies of amino acid sequences in proteins, such as cytochrome c and fibrinogen, are also used in taxonomy.

(b) List three features that all organisms classified into the kingdom Plantae have in common, other than being eukaryotic. (3 marks)

ⓔ Do not write down the first three things that come into your head. Always think about your answers before writing anything down. Often the first things thought of are incorrect or too vague and not specific enough. 'Green' might be an answer that pops into your head. Would that get a mark?

(c) Explain the advantages of using evidence from DNA and proteins in research work in taxonomy. (4 marks)

ⓔ Think carefully about answering this question and re-read the passage to see if there is any information to help you. Do not simply repeat the information, use it to back up your argument.

Total: 8 marks

Student A

(a) Phylogeny is the evolutionary history of a species.

Student B

(a) Phylogeny is how you classify species into phyla.

ⓔ The specification states that you have to define the term phylogeny. Student A has given a crisp definition. Some learning outcomes start with the word 'Define', so you can expect to be asked to do this. A good idea is to make your own glossary of terms and then learn it thoroughly before the examination. Student B obviously has not done this. Notice how easy it is to see a word and think of the wrong definition.

Student A

(b) Multicellular. Autotrophic. Cells have cellulose cell walls.

Student B

(b) Plants carry out photosynthesis. Their cells have nuclei. Cells have large vacuoles. Plants do not move.

ⓔ Student B has given four answers. Only three are required so the examiner will mark the first three only. This is unfortunate, because the student has included the meaning of the term eukaryotic ('their cells have nuclei') so that does not count. This means that the final answer ('plants do not move'), which is correct, does not gain a mark. Student B gains 2 marks.

Student A

(c) It can be difficult to tell closely related species apart especially if you cannot breed them together to see if they produce fertile offspring. Often this is impossible because there are not enough specimens, the specimens have been collected in the wild and are now dead, the specimens have been preserved for a long time or they are fossil species. Over time, the sequence of bases (A, C, G and T) in genes changes. Often this has no effect on the sequence of amino acids in proteins. By comparing the sequence of nucleotides and sequence of amino acids between two different species, you can tell how closely related they are.

Student B

(c) Scientists have compared the amino acid sequences (primary structure) of proteins like haemoglobin, fibrinogen and cytochrome c. Animals that are closely related (e.g. chimpanzee and humans) show no or very few differences. Animals that are less closely related have many more differences. This information is helpful to confirm classifications based on other features. But DNA sequences are more varied than primary sequences as most amino acids are coded for by more than one triplet. So there are more differences in DNA sequences and by comparing the sequence of nucleotides you get even more data about differences and similarities between species.

ⓔ Both answers gain full marks. This is quite a difficult topic for you to appreciate in full at this stage. The differences between the DNA and proteins are due to mutation, which is a topic covered at A2. However, it is appropriate for now to consider the sequences of bases in DNA and the sequences of amino acids in proteins. Both students have explained this well, with student B giving some examples of proteins that have been sequenced and used in taxonomic studies. DNA barcoding of animals uses a gene from mitochondrial DNA. You will learn more about this at A2.

ⓔ **Student B gets 6 marks out of 8 for Question 7.**

Question 8 **Maintaining biodiversity**

The Society Islands of French Polynesia in the Pacific, including Tahiti and Moorea, have a rich biodiversity, including many endemic species that are not found anywhere else. Studies of the different species of the land snail genus *Partula* revealed how much diversity can evolve on islands. However, by the end of the twentieth century, the number of species on the Society Islands had fallen from 61 to 5.

- **The east African giant land snail, *Achatina fulica*, was introduced to many islands in the Pacific during the Second World War as a food source for American troops.**
- **The giant land snails escaped and became a pest, eating farmers' crops.**
- **The predatory rosy wolf snail, *Euglandina rosea*, was introduced to control the giant land snail.**

- ***E. rosea* preyed on the much smaller *Partula* species, driving many to extinction.**
- **Specimens of several *Partula* species were rescued by conservationists and kept in zoos in Europe and America.**

The International Partula Conservation Programme is using *ex situ* and *in situ* methods to conserve the biodiversity of this group of land snails.

Suggest suitable conservation methods that may protect the *Partula* species.

ⓔ There is a lot to read and think about here. This means that there will be marks available for using the information given in the answer. Make notes before you start writing the answer and plan what you intend to put into each paragraph.

Total: 8 marks

Student A

The five species of snail that are not extinct need to be protected, perhaps by setting up reserves for them so they are protected in their habitat. This is *in situ* conservation as it happens in the snails' habitat. It would involve controlling the predatory snail. Measures to remove both introduced species from the areas around the reserves would reduce chances of the predatory snail migrating into the reserves. Local people may have to be told about the importance of local biodiversity and recruited to help protect the snails and stop habitat destruction. New habitats for the snails could be created. Groups of snails at risk could be moved to reserves, perhaps on other islands. Snails kept in zoos could be used for *ex situ* conservation and used in breeding programmes. The zoos would have to make sure that inbreeding did not occur as that often weakens the species. They could do this by exchanging snails or their sperm and eggs. When there are enough snails, some could be reintroduced to the wild.

Student B

There are different ways to protect endangered animals from extinction:

- habitat destruction, such as deforestation, can be halted
- nature reserves can be created
- animals can be put on the endangered list
- trade in animals is prevented by CITES
- biodiversity action plans can be written

The *Partula* snails need to be protected against their predators, so these could be excluded from the habitat, perhaps by putting some sort of snail-proof fence around a reserve, as farmers do with rabbits. It is better to protect species in their natural habitat if possible. Laws can be made to stop people destroying areas of the habitat. Development work (e.g. building of roads, houses) must be assessed by biologists in case it would remove the habitat of these snails, as happens in the UK with EIAs.

ⓔ The examiner has hinted that candidates may use the terms *in situ* and *ex situ* in their answers. Student B has not followed this hint. He/she has ignored *ex situ* conservation and could have mentioned the breeding programmes that student A has referred to. Student A has made good use of the stimulus material in the question. Student B has used bullet points in the answer. It is quite acceptable to use bullet points for these long answers, so long as each one is informative and a complete sentence. In this case only the first two would gain marks but would be better with some more detail. Both candidates could have referred to other examples of conservation to illustrate their answers. In this case a reference to trade in animals (CITES) is unlikely to be appropriate as it is not a form of *ex situ* or *in situ* conservation. Legal protection and EIAs are just about acceptable here as they are involved in protecting habitats for the snails. Student B should have given the full name – environmental impact assessments – but often examiners will give marks if names are not written out in full. It is acceptable to write CITES, for example, rather than have to remember its full name. Student B gains 5 marks.

You can read more about this example of international conservation by looking at the websites of two English zoos involved in rescuing *Partula* species from extinction: **www.zsl.org and www.bristolzoo.org**. You can search the IUCN red data list for all the threatened *Partula* species at **www.iucnredlist.org**.

Student B gets 5 marks out of 8 for Question 8.

Overall, Student B gains 35 marks.

You can see that Student B has lost marks for a number of different reasons.

- Changes to answers are not made clearly enough, e.g. Q.1(a).
- Technical terms are spelt incorrectly, e.g. Q.1(b)(i).
- Some answers are not developed fully, e.g. Q.1(d), Q.4(c).
- Appropriate terms have not been used, e.g. Q.2(c), Q.3(c), Q.5(a).
- Definitions have not been given correctly, e.g. Q.2(b) and Q.7(a).
- Terms have not been named in full, e.g. EIAs in Q.8.
- Instructions have not been followed carefully, e.g. Q.1(a) and (b)(ii), Q.5(c), Q.7(b).
- Data provided have not been used in answers, e.g. Q.3(a)(ii), Q.5(a) and (c), Q.6(d).
- Data provided have not been quoted accurately, e.g. Q.5(b).
- Answers are not precise enough, e.g. Q.3(b), where the student uses the word 'amount' rather than 'volume' and Q.3(d), where detailed steps are required.
- Calculations are not carried out correctly, e.g. Q.4(a) and Q.6(a).
- Answers are too general and need more development, e.g. Q.2(b) and (c), Q.3(c), Q.5(c), Q.6(d), Q.8.
- Information is copied incorrectly from the question paper, e.g. Q.1(b)(ii) and Q.3(d), where calcium ions are ignored.
- Common errors have been made, e.g. Q.1(d), where active sites and substrates are said to have the same shape; referring to size when the question asks about structure in Q.1(e); writing 'iodine' instead of 'iodine solution' or 'iodine in potassium iodide solution' in Q.3(d); adding iodine solution to the reaction mixture containing amylase in Q.3(d); giving the axes of a graph the wrong way around in Q.3(d).
- Irrelevant material is included, e.g. Q.4(b)(ii) and (c), Q.5(c) and Q.8.
- In Q.2 it is clear that student B has neglected to learn the biochemistry of DNA in Module 1. This is an important topic that underpins much of the work in this Unit and many topics in Unit F215 at A2.

Knowledge check answers

1 There are 20 different amino acids used to make proteins. These can be arranged in any order to give the huge variety of proteins.

2

Feature	Haemoglobin	Collagen
Type of protein	Globular	Fibrous
Soluble in water	Yes	No
Number of polypeptides	Four	Three
Prosthetic group	Haem	None
Function	Transport oxygen and carbon dioxide	Provide strength to tissues, e.g. ligaments and tendons

3 In α-glucose the –H is above the –OH on carbon 1; in β-glucose it is the reverse.

4 Any three from: α-glucose has a ring structure, no nitrogen, no –R group, no –C=O group.

5 Maltose — α-glucose; sucrose — fructose and α-glucose; glycogen — α-glucose; amylopectin — α-glucose; amylose — α-glucose; cellulose — β-glucose.

6 A triglyceride is not a polymer; not branched; contains at least two different sub-unit molecules (glycogen is made from α-glucose only); contains ester bonds (not glycosidic bonds).

7 They are charged and water soluble, so they cannot pass through the phospholipid bilayer. They pass through protein channels or carriers that have hydrophilic cores.

8

Test substance	Reagent	Details of test	Positive result	Negative result
Starch	Iodine solution	Add to solid or to a solution	Blue-black colour	Yellow colour
Reducing sugar	Benedict's reagent	Add to a solution; boil (or put at > 80°C)	Green, yellow, orange, red colour with precipitate	No change to blue colour; no precipitate
Non-reducing sugar	Hydrochloric acid; sodium hydroxide solution Benedict's solution	Sample 1 – as for reducing sugar Sample 2 – boil with HCl and then neutralise with NaOH; boil with Benedict's solution	Sample 1 – no change to blue colour (if no reducing sugars) Sample 2 – green, yellow, orange, red colour with precipitate	Both samples — no colour change
Protein	Biuret solution	Add to a solution	Violet/lilac/purple	No change to blue colour
Fat	Ethanol	Dissolve test substance in ethanol, then pour into water	Cloudy emulsion	No emulsion

9 DNA: contains deoxyribose, not ribose; contains thymine, not uracil; is double-stranded, not single-stranded.

10 Nucleotides of new polynucleotide are assembled against the template strand by base pairing: A–T, T–A, C–G and G–C.

11 Enzymes are proteins that are made by cells; catalysts increase rates of chemical reactions; lower activation energy; remain unchanged at the end of reactions.

12 There is so much variation possible by assembling the 20 different amino acids to give 'pockets' lined by –R-groups that act as active sites. This is not possible with polysaccharides because they are made from very few monomers; the polysaccharides covered in this unit are each made from only one monomer — glucose.

13 A competitive inhibitor fits into the active site thereby blocking entry of the substrate; a non-competitive inhibitor fits into another part of the enzyme molecule leading to a change in the shape of the active site so that it can no longer accept a substrate molecule.

14 Cholesterol molecules are transported in the centre of a lipoprotein surrounded by proteins and phospholipids which have their hydrophilic regions facing the outside and interacting with water.

15 To prevent the selection of antibiotic-resistant bacteria that may enter the human food chain and infect people. Many antibiotics are becoming ineffective because of antibiotic resistance in bacteria, so the ban was introduced to make sure that antibiotics remain effective.

16 Memory cells enable a fast response during the secondary immune response to an antigen. This prevents infection by pathogens with the same antigen from causing disease.

17 Secondary response is faster and involves production of a higher concentration of antibodies than the primary response.

18 Active immunity involves an immune response; production of antibodies within the body; formation of memory cells. None of these things happens in passive immunity. The primary response in active immunity is slower than in passive immunity; active immunity provides long-term protection, passive immunity is temporary.

19 Influenza antigens change from year to year as a result of mutation and 'cross-breeding' between strains of influenza viruses. The body does not recognise these new antigens and so immunity to previous infections or vaccinations does not provide protection against new strains.

20 An antibiotic is a medicinal drug used to treat bacterial diseases (they are not effective against viruses). An antibody is a protein secreted by activated B lymphocytes (plasma cells) on stimulation by an antigen.

21 Tar contains carcinogens that cause mutations; mutation(s) occurs in an epithelial cell lining the bronchus; mutation of genes that control cell division results in uncontrolled mitosis; this takes a long time to produce a group of undifferentiated cells (a tumour); this grows into the lung tissues blocking airways and blood vessels.

22 Epidemiological evidence may show a correlation, but cannot prove cause and effect.

23 Species richness is the number of species present in an area. Species evenness is the abundance of the different species in an area.

24 Taxon: a group used in classification, e.g. kingdom, class and species. Hierarchy: a system of organisation in which each group is subdivided into further groups — for example a kingdom is divided into classes, each class is divided into orders, etc. Binomial system: system for naming organisms consisting of the genus name and the specific name. Phylogeny: the evolutionary history of a taxon, e.g. a species.

25 3; 5. Causes may be genetic (e.g. mutation to form new alleles) and/or environmental (e.g. food availability to support growth).

26 A feature (physiological, behavioural, etc.) that helps an organism 'fit' into its habitat, breed and pass on its alleles.

27 Species richness and evenness; genetic diversity within species; ecosystem diversity.